A Sound Approach to Teaching Instrumentalists

SECOND EDITION

A Sound Approach to Teaching Instrumentalists

An Application of Content and Learning Sequences

STANLEY L. SCHLEUTER

Australia • Canada • Mexico • Singapore • Spain • United Kingdom • United States

Schirmer is an imprint of the Wadsworth Group,
a division of Thomson Learning, Inc.
Thomson Learning™ is a trademark
used herein under license.

Wadsworth Group/Thomson Learning
10 Davis Drive
Belmont CA 94002-3098
USA

For information about our products, contact us:
Thomson Learning Academic Resource Center
1-800-423-0563
http://www.wadsworth.com

For permission to use material from this text, contact us by
Web: http://www.thomsonrights.com
Fax: 1-800-730-2215
Phone: 1-800-730-2214

Printed in the United States of America
10 9 8 7 6 5 4 3

Library of Congress Cataloging-in-Publication Data
Schleuter, Stanley L.
    A sound approach to teaching instrumentalists : an application of content
and learning sequences / Stanley L. Schleuter. — 2nd ed.
       p.   cm.
    Includes bibliographical references and index.
    ISBN 0-02-864716-5
    1. Instrumental music—Instruction and study. I. Title.
MT170.S34   1996
784.193'07—dc20   96-42540
                                           CIP
                                           MN

This paper meets the requirements of ANSI/NISO Z39.48-1992 (Permanence of
Paper).

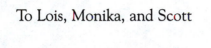

To Lois, Monika, and Scott

Contents

1. An Overview of Past and Current Practices

2. The Process of Learning Music

3. Teaching a Sense of Tonality

4. Teaching Rhythmic Feeling

5. Teaching Performance Skills through Pattern Vocabularies and Music

6. Some Aspects of the Teaching Process

7. Assessment of Music Achievement and Music Aptitude

Preface

Instrumental music is an important force in the musical culture of this country. Thousands of children learn to play instruments in our schools every year, but many instrumental teachers, because of training or instructional philosophy, attend primarily to the technical skills of instrumental performance. School instrumental music programs often give more attention to group performance levels than to individual musical development. The result is that school instrumental music programs are often criticized because a majority of instrumentalists lack musical independence and, in many cases, musicianship.

There is increasing interest in implementing standards of music achievement throughout K–12 music offerings. This is exemplified by the voluntary national standards for school music recently published and advocated by the Music Educators National Conference. Teachers of instrumentalists will be held even more accountable for what is taught about music knowledge and performance practice in addition to instrument technique. Since the 1970s there has been an increasing interest in a comprehensive musicianship approach to school instrumental performance groups, where the music serves to teach a curriculum of both knowledge and skills.

What is this book about? This book examines the application of musical content and learning sequences to teaching instrumental music to students from elementary school through adult ages. A basic premise is that music consists primarily of tonal and rhythmic content and that instrumental teaching and learning can best be accomplished through an expression of musical content and ideas. Teachers are encouraged to have open minds and to be eclectic in their choice of materials and techniques. Efficient learning and teaching can occur when musical content and learning skills are properly sequenced. The aim of the approach described in this book is to meet individual student needs and differences of musical achievement usually within group instructional settings.

This book supplies material that is typically omitted from "comprehensive" texts for instrumental music education classes. The book's content centers around teaching tonal and rhythmic understandings while developing instrumental technique. The aim is to develop students who have something to perform rather than students who just perform something. Such specific technical information as fingering charts, bowings, embouchure, or hand positions for various instruments is intentionally omitted from this book. Nor does this book include discussions on how to organize a music library, prepare for a performance trip, develop a budget, and so on. Such information is widely available in other sources.

The book is organized into seven chapters. Chapter 1 is a brief chronology of teaching instrumental music in the schools of this country. Major influences on the development of school instrumental music programs are discussed and current trends are described. Chapter 2 provides contributions of selected psychologists and educators, with current knowledge about learning processes as a proposed basis for teaching instrumental music. Developing a sense of tonality and a tonal pattern vocabulary is discussed in Chapter 3, which includes tonal content sequence and teaching techniques. A list of tonal objectives in a sequence of learning is provided. Chapter 4 deals with the concept of developing a sense of rhythmic feeling and a rhythm pattern vocabulary. Rhythm readiness, content sequence, and teaching techniques are also discussed. A list of rhythm objectives in a sequence of learning is provided. How to acquire instrumental performance skills while learning tonal and rhythm pattern vocabularies and other music content is explained in Chapter 5. Learning sequence is used as a basis for diagnosing musical problems and arriving at solutions; lesson examples are included. Chapter 6 presents information, most of it research based, about how we can improve the effectiveness of our teaching. This chapter is new with this edition of the book. Finally, Chapter 7 provides measurement techniques for tonal, rhythmic, and instrument skill objectives. The chapter includes discussion of rating scales, teacher-made tests, portfolios, and standardized tests and describes techniques for reporting instrumental achievement.

Who should read this book? This book should be of help to anyone who plans to teach or currently teaches instrumentalists. Studio teachers of private lessons will also benefit, although most of the discussions refer to teaching beginning through advanced instrumentalists in school settings. The book is appropriate for undergraduate and graduate instrumental music majors, studio teachers, and especially school music teachers.

How can this book help you? Your efficiency as a teacher should be improved by following the sequences for tonal and rhythmic content. You should be able to organize musical objectives as a basis for teaching instruments and meeting the needs of individual students. Your skills in diagnosing problems and prescribing solutions should improve. Most of all, your students should become more musical and independent as instrumentalists.

Teaching will not necessarily become easier as you improve your diagnostic and prescriptive skills. Instead, the process increases in complexity. The demands on the teacher for flexibility and conceptualizing of musical content, materials, and teaching techniques will increase. You will no longer be satisfied with requiring all students to do the same thing at the same time or simply to follow the page chronology of an instruction book. The end result, however, will be the increasing rewards of developing musically functional students who gradually become independent of their music teachers and who have something to say and perform with their instruments.

A few additional thoughts for this revised edition are included here. Since completing the first edition of the book about fifteen years ago, it is gratifying to hear of the successes that many students in this and other countries have had after studying and implementing much of the content and ideas. I continue to learn from my students also and hope the expansion of content, ideas, and specific teaching examples in this edition will be even more helpful to conscientious instrumental music teachers in schools and studios. Our students can only benefit if we seek to learn as we teach.

S. S.

List of Figures

List of Tables

CHAPTER 1

An Overview of Past and Current Practices

The teaching of instrumental music in the schools of this country is a relatively recent phenomenon. It began in the mid-1800s and was not widespread until after World War I. The rapid growth in the number of students involved in instrumental music programs in schools is a tribute to many dedicated music teachers of the past eighty years. How and what students are taught has also developed over the years as students' needs and expectations have evolved.

Early Efforts

Until the late 1800s, music teaching in our schools consisted mainly of vocal instruction. Private teachers provided instrument instruction through individual and class lessons outside of public school settings, the most popular instrument being the piano. Teachers, instrumental teaching methods, and materials frequently originated in Europe; however, a few exceptions can be documented in various communities. The Benjamins taught violin classes in their music academies in New York, Pennsylvania, and New Jersey during the last half of the nineteenth century. They published instructional materials, sold instruments, organized concerts, and started hundreds of students on instruments (Sollinger, 1970, chap. 15).

Birge ([1928, 1939] 1966) lists four reasons for the increased impetus of school music instruction that occurred during the last half of the nineteenth century: 1) the growing influence and professional recognition of private music teachers, 2) the proliferation of choral groups and festivals, 3) the formation of professional symphony orchestras and professional bands, and 4) the establishment of college music courses and music conservatories.

In addition, community bands and orchestras gained in popularity during the late 1800s and influenced public support for school groups. Outdoor band concerts in parks became a popular form of entertainment, and bands were often formed by town governments, factories, and colleges but rarely by public schools. By the mid-1850s it was common for towns of any size to have a community band. Instruments and instruction manuals were available through the mail. Band members studied their instruments with private teachers, or sometimes were self-taught. In this preelectronic media era, these instrumental ensembles were important sources of entertainment and offered opportunities for musicians to perform. These groups undoubtedly motivated many children to learn to play an instrument. Schools began responding by offering more instrumental training. An example of the thinking of the period comes from the 1880 edition of McCosh's *Guide for Amateur Brass Bands*:

> While the study of music educates the mind, it helps to purify and refine the character. . . . [T]he most practical way of indulging a taste for the arts is in the organization of a brass band. . . . A Brass Band, it is true, in its commencement, may be termed a noisy organization, but all music was evolved from the chaos of sound by the discovering mind of man. . . . So it will be after a time with a Band. Its members will learn to master their instruments, and blow gentle notes of sweet melodies, instead of the harsh sounds that come from inexperienced lips. Thus, through the energy of perseverance, a lovely result may follow (Bryant, 1975, p. 21).

School orchestras and bands were established intermittently between 1850 and the end of the century, in states from Kansas to Massachusetts. An example at the end of this period is the Richmond, Indiana, school orchestra that began in 1898 under the direction of Will Earhart. Instrumentations of school bands and orchestras were diverse. Bands contained various stringed instruments, and orchestras might include any instruments available. Groups were often made up of no more than ten to twelve members. Students continued to learn how to play instruments from private teachers, and group rehearsals usually were held outside of regular school hours.

Acceptance of school instrumental programs grew slowly. During the last half of the nineteenth century, several key events helped promote the need and desire for such programs. First, instrumentalists from military bands of the Civil War became teachers. Military music was so popular during the Civil War that the Union Army put a limit on the number of military bands. After the war, bandsmen scattered across the country; many subsequently served as conductors of school or community groups. They also taught private lessons and performed in community groups.

Second, musical instruments improved technologically, and more were manufactured in this country. The Boehm fingering system was introduced on clarinets and flutes. The saxophone family gained in popularity. Piston valves became the standard on most brass instruments.

Third, professional orchestras and bands were organized and began to standardize instrumentations. Between 1842 and 1900, major professional orchestras were formed in New York, Boston, Chicago, St. Louis, Cincinnati, and Philadelphia.

Fourth, touring bands and orchestras visited towns and cities throughout the country and helped create the impetus for forming school and community instrumental groups. One of the earliest important touring groups was the orchestra conducted by Theodore Thomas, who later founded the Chicago Symphony Orchestra. Other touring professional bands included those conducted by Patrick Gilmore and Frederick Innes, and the most famous of all was the John Philip Sousa Band. Sousa first began touring the country as conductor of the United States Marine Band in 1891. He later established his own civilian band that traversed the country by railroad. These live performances brought contemporary music by European and American composers to the masses. Professional touring groups were influential and active well past the turn of the century.

Fifth, the phenomenal growth in numbers of public high schools (from about 300 in 1860 to about 6,000 by 1900) provided settings for future instruction of instruments. Finally, John Dewey's "learn by doing" philosophy of education began to have a wide influence in school curricula, by diminishing the classical orientation of curricula and encouraging students to participate and experience in order to learn.

Major Influences in the 1900s

At least four major factors continued the spread of school instrumental music during the first three decades of this century. The first of these was World War I. Service bands were used extensively for ceremonial purposes and to entertain troops and rally patriots. The federal government hired famous musicians, such as Walter and Frank Damrosch and Percy Grainger, to train military musicians. The military became a large and important market for instrument manufacturers. Following the war, many bandsmen and conductors became music teachers in the schools, and the music instrument industry eventually worked to develop school music as a new marketplace. Touring bands continued to travel throughout the country. On the cover of a September 1917 edition of *Musical Truth*, published by the instrument manufacturer C. G. Conn, are pictures of "Seven of the Most Prominent Bandmasters of America"—Patrick Conway, Arthur Pryor, Bohumir Kryl, John Philip Sousa, Guiseppe Creatore, Frederick Innes, and A. Liberati. From the 1920s on, more and more school orchestras and bands were formed that rehearsed during the school day, were financed by school funds, and were directed by a full-time school music teacher.

The second major influence was the formation in 1907 of the Music Supervisors National Conference (MSNC), which became the Music Educators National Conference (MENC) in 1934. Although mainly concerned with vocal music in its early years, by the 1920s and 1930s this organization served to promote school instrumental music across the country through publicity, teacher conventions, and teacher training clinics. Outstanding school instrumental organizations performed at many of the conventions and did much to convince teachers and school administrators of the potential for school instrumental music. For example, the Richmond, Indiana, high school orchestra conducted by Joseph Maddy performed a concert that was particularly well received at the 1922 MSNC meeting, and soon after, the Committee on Instrumental Affairs was formed. The Committee had impact nationally by recommending instrumentation standards and by publishing lists of literature, disseminating teaching methods and ideas, and organizing competitions.

The third major reason for the growing numbers of school instrumentalists was the national contest movement. Various competitions for instrumental music groups had existed around the country for at least fifty years. The School Band Contest of America was organized in 1923 as a promotional device by instrument manufacturers. In the same year, the Committee on Instrumental Affairs of the Music Supervisors National Conference took control of the contest and reorganized the rules and format, with the first national school band contest occurring in 1926 in Fostoria, Ohio, and the first national school orchestra contest following in 1929 in Iowa City, Iowa. The contests grew in popularity each year until they ended with the 1940 competitions after the outbreak of World War II. With the momentum interrupted, they were never scheduled again following the war. The contest activities helped delimit the instrumentation of school bands and orchestras and directed attention to providing appropriate music for school groups. Thousands of students participated in the competitions, representing their schools and communities. The numbers of school instrumental teachers and quality of instruction grew accordingly, and public support for school instrumental music reached new heights. Instrument manufacturers became convinced that school instrumental music was the market of the future. Performance levels, published music, and instrumentation concepts all benefited from the contest movement.

Fourth and perhaps most important as an influence on the proliferation of school instrumental music was the development of class instruction techniques and materials. Teaching instruments to groups of students was not a new idea. It was the typical mode of instruction in European music conservatories, where students of similar abilities were grouped in various-sized classes and then performed for each other to perfect technique. Although the European patterns of instruction were brought to this country and used in music conservatories, classes tended to be smaller and private lessons were still preferred. Class instruction in public schools included the procedures for teaching an entire band or orchestra in one heterogeneous group from beginning through advanced levels. New materials and techniques evolved. Free class lessons in schools were the keys to involving the masses of students needed to complete the growing instrumentations of the orchestras and bands. Class lesson techniques became the mass production device for instrumental music. As class lessons were introduced, grade school bands and orchestras became commonplace and served as training grounds and "feeders" for high school groups.

Class Methods

Early efforts to teach classes of beginners in this country occurred in private music classes and academies. Lewis Benjamin, Sr., wrote *The Musical Academy* for his stringed instrument classes in 1851. His sons, Lewis, Jr., and Frank, organized the Benjamin Brothers Musical Academy in Brooklyn, New York, and during the 1880s and 1890s enjoyed success as teachers of instrument classes, authors of materials, and sellers of instruments. The *New Class Book* was written by Joseph Howell in about 1859 for violin classes in Arkansas (Sollinger, 1970, pp. 272–278).

The first widespread instrument class instruction in schools of this country was for classes of violins. Charles Farnsworth visited England in 1908 and observed that thousands of English children were being taught violin by class instruction in what became known as the Maidstone movement (Deverich, 1987). Knowing of Farnsworth's discovery, Albert Mitchell, an accomplished musician trained in England and a Boston music teacher, visited England in 1910 to study the class lesson techniques being employed to teach violin to masses of children. After returning to this country and successfully experimenting with the process, Mitchell (1924) developed and published the *Class Method for Violin*. It was adapted later for other instruments. The *Instrumental Music Course* by Benjamin Stuber (1923) was another violin class method published at about the same time. New techniques for teaching and managing class groups of instrumentalists continued to evolve rapidly during the 1920s and 1930s; the reference list at the end of this chapter provides additional sources of detail on these methods.

Teaching classes of mixed instrumentations received great impetus from Joseph Maddy and Thaddeus Giddings (1923) with the publication of *The Universal Teacher*. This material permitted even more flexibility with heterogeneous groups of instruments. The method emphasized melodic rather than technical drill material for all instruments. Students were expected to also sing the melodies and transpose by ear, and harmonizations of some melodies were included. *The Universal Teacher* was a model for future instruction materials developed for school instrumentalists.

Class instrumental instruction became predominant soon after the dissemination of usable instructional materials in schools. Although private lessons continued in many schools, class instruction was considered by many to have advantages. Theodore Normann (1941, pp. 142–144) discussed five such advantages:

1. It opens the way to all children to discover their talent and interest in music by offering instruction at little or no cost
2. Class instruction socializes the music lesson by encouraging cooperation, self-reliance, and good sportsmanship
3. The mortality is lower because of the increased opportunities to stimulate and maintain interest
4. Class teaching permits and encourages a rich and extensive musicianship by correlating previous music study in the schoolroom with eartraining, design, sight-reading, ensemble-playing, and the like
5. Class instruction enables the director to develop and maintain a symphonic instrumentation. From the class group the director can choose according to the needs of his organization.

Besides class instruction for school band and orchestral instruments, group piano lessons were popular in many schools during the 1920s and 1930s.

Method Book Content

The two types of class methods—like and mixed instruments—continue to the present. Method books are published for individual lessons also, and emphasize characteristic studies for specific instruments. Individual instrument method books formerly contained mostly technical drill exercises and very little material of melodic interest. Current class methods are the reverse and use a majority of melodic material. Training material for technique is often available in supplementary books.

Drill and technique material was generally emphasized in like-instrument methods such as the *Rubank Elementary Method* (1934), in contrast to heterogeneous class methods. Exercises are mainly brief studies emphasizing chords, scales, rhythms, articulations, and fingering technique.

Fingering charts and occasionally pictures of embouchure, hand positions, and posture were included in most early materials designed for class instruction. Later publications followed similar formats.

Rhythm notation is the underlying organizer in nearly all instrument method books. This may be due to the pervasive influence of early piano training materials. Almost all authors organize their material around proportionality of note values beginning with whole notes and rests, then progressing through half, quarter, and sixteenth notes and rests. Mathematical and visual connotations of note values are stressed. The basic rhythmic difference among the various methods is the pacing of new materials and the amount of material presented that emphasizes each note value. Various counting systems are included (1-e-and-a most often) and are always simultaneously introduced with the notation. If any correlated physical movement is advocated, it is usually foot-tapping. The assumption is that students do not have or need rhythm readiness activities before learning music notation. It is also assumed that longer note values are easier to play and read than shorter note values.

Most methods contain no directed material or information for developing a sense of tonality. Nearly all melodies are in major mode and, especially in more recent books, are limited to a few keys. Arpeggio and chord studies are usually intended as fingering or articulation exercises rather than as tonality training. The inclusion of much melodic material indirectly aids the development of a sense of tonality.

Between 1940 and about 1970, many new class method books were published; their content, however, was basically variations of the content and sequence in earlier method books. Changes are often mainly cosmetic rather than based on advances in understanding how music is learned. A few innovations in content appeared during the 1970s. Some method books, such as *Take One* by Charles Peters and Matt Betton (1972), contain material in jazz idioms. *The Individualized Instructor* and the more recent series *Listen, Move, Sing, and Play* by James O. Froseth (1970, 1982) are particularly noteworthy in that rhythm training is systematically introduced without using the proportional note value approach. The content sequence is research based. Both series make extensive use of melodic rounds and include words with familiar songs.

With few exceptions, most instrumental class method books that have appeared over the past half century emphasize 1) the primary association of fingerings with notation rather than sound; 2) the mathematics of proportional note values; 3) note naming; and 4) a mixture of technical and melodic material. Materials and techniques are infrequently correlated with classroom general music beyond the coincidence of a few songs. Although thousands of students continue to be trained with these materials, there are many possibilities to improve instructional practices based on current research and innovations.

Other Developments

Many other developments have enhanced or changed teaching techniques and materials during the past seventy years of school instrumental music training programs. Colleges and universities have established elaborate degree programs and requirements for instrumental music education students who wish to teach in public schools. Music teacher training degrees, most of which began as two-year programs, have expanded to four and even five years of study for a bachelor's degree. Courses of study typically include instruction in teaching techniques, materials, conducting, and instrument skills besides music theory, music history, applied instrument study, general studies, and generic education courses.

Marching bands, concert bands, jazz ensembles, symphony orchestras, and string orchestras are commonly found in colleges and universities. These organizations often approach or reach professional levels of proficiency and become models for high school groups. College and military instrumental groups have helped to fill the void left by the demise of professional touring bands and orchestras. Instrumentations, performance styles, and demands for compositions and arrangements are today directly influenced by college and military performance groups.

Most state requirements for teacher certification now permit only certified music graduates to teach instrumental music in public schools. State requirements usually determine the emphases in undergraduate curricula for training music teachers. The number of instrumental music teachers available for school positions continues to increase during this century.

Repertoire available for teaching instrumentalists has grown considerably in quantity and quality. Publishers of method books often have a catalog of supplementary materials ranging from beginning to advanced levels, typically including instruction on solos for all instruments, small and large ensembles, technical drills, and selections for full band or orchestra. Composers and arrangers have capitalized on the needs of school instrumentalists. Newly composed music in a variety of styles is available to all.

The main emphasis in school instrumental music programs continues to be large-group performances, particularly at the secondary level. Participation in grade school and middle school or junior high school music performance groups is often considered as preparatory training for participation in high school groups. Class lessons in many schools are primarily concerned with preparing the music for the band or orchestra. The most common school instrumental groups—orchestras, concert bands, and marching bands—are established as early as the elementary grades.

Since the creation of band halftime shows for University of Illinois football games near the turn of the century, school marching bands have become increasingly popular because of their public visibility in parades, festivals, and football halftime shows. These groups often become the main display unit of instrumental music programs in schools. Although marching bands should emphasize musical development, they are often criticized for ignoring musical objectives and for performing a very limited repertoire.

Schools have been criticized too for overemphasizing instrumental performing groups that involve less than 10 percent of the total secondary-school population. The Music Educators National Conference (MENC 1986) has published guidelines for types and frequencies of performances. MENC is also active in publishing courses of study for strings, winds, and percussion; repertoire lists; and manuals for beginning teachers (MENC, 1991a, 1991b; Mayer, 1993; Fleming, 1994; Reul, 1994; Zerull, 1994).

At the middle, junior high, and high school levels, many schools stress availability of instrumental learning opportunities for any student who wishes to participate rather than offering groups for only a few select trained instrumentalists. Beginning-class piano instruction is generating renewed interest primarily because of the development of inexpensive and reliable electronic keyboards that may be integrated with computer technology. Other offerings include guitar classes, synthesizer classes, and steel drum bands.

Electronic technology and computer applications are having an increasing impact on instrumental music instruction in schools. Computer assisted instruction (CAI) is becoming pervasive as hardware and software are developed and become practical for school use. Software is available to teach instrument fingerings, tuning, notation, composition, terminology, and many other aspects of music. New instruments and sounds are available that depend on computer interaction. Computer-performed accompaniments are available that follow the tempo and nuances as a soloist practices or performs. The latest technology incorporates visual and audio aspects through compact discs and computers.

Jazz ensembles also continue to increase in popularity in middle, junior, and high schools. They perform a variety of popular music styles including jazz, rock and roll, and swing. The inclusion of styles of music that incorporate improvisation is appealing to many students.

Small instrumental ensemble activity may also be found in schools at all levels. Solo and ensemble contests and evaluation festivals often act as stimuli for the formation of small ensembles, and students are exposed to another vast repertoire for their instruments. Guy Kinney (1981) and other writers emphasize that small-ensemble performance is an excellent method to develop musicianship, instrumental technique, and positive attitudes toward music.

Many instrumental teachers are now being held accountable for individual student achievement of musical objectives in addition to the accomplishments of group performance. Besides preparing selections for the next concert, rehearsals may include such activities as directed listening, analysis, composition, and arranging. The comprehensive musicianship approach to training instrumentalists has had a positive effect since its development in the 1960s. It centers on choosing quality music for performance and integrating knowledge about the music within group rehearsals. Garofalo (1983a, 1983b) has authored several publications for implementing comprehensive musicianship in school bands. Developing musically educated students through performance is an overall goal.

School instrumental music curricula and staffing, meanwhile, have suffered from the growing unwillingness or inability to adequately fund the programs with tax money. Many programs could not exist without extra financial support from parents and the community. Rohner (1995) in *The Instrumentalist* magazine reports in their annual survey of school instrumental music budgets that nontax dollars (fund-raising) accounts for 63 percent of high school instrumental music funding and 39 percent for elementary and junior high school levels. The combined amount attributed to fund-raising across grade levels is 56 percent for the 1994–1995 school year. Although the total amount of money from all sources increases most years, the proportion coming from fund-raising also increases. Nationally, enrollment in school instrumental music tends to increase slightly each year. Fiscal constraints have a negative impact on the music programs in many communities.

Instrumental music instruction in schools in this country owes much of its heritage to western European musical styles, music conservatory techniques, and music materials. Curriculums are usually slow in adapting innovations and change. One important curriculum influence in the past thirty years is the approach to teaching stringed instruments adapted from Shinichi Suzuki's Talent Education method from Japan. Elements of Suzuki's program that have some acceptance in this country include beginning instruction with children as early as three years old, extensive listening of recordings of all music to be learned, parental involvement and supervision of home practice times, and carefully sequenced steps to develop instrument technique (Suzuki, 1969).

A current curriculum influence that is just beginning to affect instrumental programs is the national attention to multicultural music in our schools. School music materials are becoming increasingly diverse and eclectic as they are drawn from the rich mixture of world musics. Recent writings by Schmid (1992), Volk (1993), Elliott (1995, pp. 207–212), and others provide background and ideas for incorporating music from many cultures in the instrumental music program.

The recent publication of the *National Standards for Arts Education* (MENC 1994, 26–29, 42–45, 59–63) may have an important effect on what music content is incorporated in school instrumental music offerings. Nine voluntary national standards are proposed for grades K–12:

1. Singing, alone and with others, a varied repertoire of music
2. Performing on instruments, alone and with others, a varied reper-toire of music
3. Improvising melodies, variations, and accompaniments
4. Composing and arranging music within specified guidelines
5. Reading and notating music
6. Listening to, analyzing, and describing music
7. Evaluating music and music performances
8. Understanding relationships between music, the other arts, and disciplines outside the arts
9. Understanding music in relation to history and culture

These standards are widely disseminated among school administrators, music teachers, and teacher trainers. Many states are incorporating them in curriculum guides for school adoption.

Recruiting Beginners

Recruitment of beginning instrumentalists has always been an impor-tant part of school instrumental music programs. Much has been writ-ten about recommended procedures (Froseth, 1971; Brown, 1985). Instrument manufacturers provide free advice and materials along with promotional "tests" (Selmer, n.d.). The National Association of Band Instrument Manufacturers (NABIM) published a pamphlet (Froseth, 1974) that offers information and suggestions. Most tradition-al recruitment depends primarily on student interest and attention-get-ting procedures. However, having a strong interest in something does not necessarily indicate or guarantee the potential to achieve. Long-term success depends more on musical aptitude and readiness than on interest.

Froseth (1971) and others demonstrated that if you want students to succeed on instruments, the best way is to initially identify those with the most potential and involve them in the program. Procedures have been refined with the publishing of legitimate music aptitude tests such as the *Musical Aptitude Profile* (Gordon, [1965] 1988) and the *Intermediate Measures of Music Audiation* (Gordon, 1982), which

may be used diagnostically to improve instruction and can aid in identifying those students who may be most likely to succeed with instrumental instruction. Another test, the *Instrument Timbre Preference Test*
(Gordon, 1984), shows some promise in identifying which instru-
ment(s) students may be most successful with by finding out their tone
quality preferences.

Even though students with high potential may demonstrate little or
no interest in playing an instrument, most will participate in a trial
period of instruction if their parents are informed that the child has
high music aptitude. Conversely, you may also have students with low
music aptitude who want to learn an instrument. Students should
never be refused instruction based on a test score.

Most school instrumentalists begin on band or orchestral instruments sometime between grades four and seven because of school patterns of staffing and building use. There is no established optimum age
for beginning to learn an instrument, although many believe that it is
important to begin before teenage years if possible. Active adults can
learn to play instruments even after retirement age.

Studies such as those by Klinedinst (1991, 1992) show that most
physical characteristics have little bearing on initial success with an
instrument. He also found that scholastic ability and academic
achievement tests are an important indicator of success and retention
for at least the first two years of instruction with grade-school students. In addition, student self-concept appears to affect attitudes
toward music and retention in instrumental programs.

Beyond School Instrumental Experiences

The fact that most instrumentalists who graduate from high school do
not continue playing their instruments is a subject of concern for many
music educators. Unfortunately, in most communities the opportunities
for adults to participate in bands and orchestras are minimal. Roth (1981,
p. 103) attributes the dearth of adult amateur bands to four factors:

1. As directors of school bands, we have devoted so much energy to
   our own groups that we have not been able to provide the leadership or expertise needed in developing successful amateur adult
   bands.

2. In some instances competition has been emphasized so strongly to our school students that musicality and the love of music has been lost. They want out.
3. In some instances school instruction has been so poor that students want no further exercises in mediocrity. Real musicianship was never developed.
4. We do not have one effective professional band organization to address the issue. Individual groups have attempted to create a central organization, but there has not been any coordinated effort.

It is also possible that more adults would be involved in instrumental music if the small ensemble and chamber music experiences were emphasized in school curricula. The desire to pursue music after graduation must be built on musicianship experiences during the school years. John P. Paynter, former conductor of the Northshore Concert Band, a well-known and long-established organization in Wilmette, Illinois, was a successful advocate of community bands and author of a manual for organizing and managing them (Paynter, 1977).

Research Efforts

Modern research and development by instrument manufacturers have resulted in better-quality instruments of all types. Acoustical research has aided instrument design. With current technology, instruments are mass produced with microtolerances in mechanism and uniform ease of playing. Instruments of high quality are manufactured so that even student-line models are reasonably priced or may be rented or leased. Schools and beginning instrumentalists can afford instruments that play well in tune, are generally easy to maintain, and are widely available.

Research efforts continue to provide useful information and suggest how the teaching of instrumentalists may be improved. Doctoral dissertations have made significant contributions, and such bibliographies as the *Woodwind Research Guide* by Lyle C. Merriman (1978) give the teacher and researcher an indication of the extent of available information. Two older publications by MENC are also of particular interest: *Teaching Performing Groups* by Charles H. Benner (1972) and

Teaching Instrumental Music by George L. Duerksen (1972). Both book-lets provide research syntheses through the early 1970s relating to instrumental instruction. More current articles and literature reviews may be regularly found in journals such as *Update*, *Journal of Band Research*, *Journal of Research in Music Education*, and *Bulletin of the Council for Research in Music Education*.

Perhaps the research most important to instrumental teaching is that concerned with how music is most efficiently and effectively learned, a topic receiving increasing interest at both the research and the developmental levels. The results often confirm or question the effectiveness of many traditional techniques and methods, and new techniques and sequences are suggested as improved teaching strate-gies. The remainder of this book is primarily concerned with how instrumental music teaching can be improved by applying what is cur-rently known about how music is learned.

Review Questions

1. What was the status of school instrumental music prior to 1850 in this country?
2. What were some of the events which helped school bands and orchestras proliferate during the last half of the nineteenth century?
3. What were some of the major influences on school instrumental music during the early 1900s?
4. Discuss the beginnings of class lesson materials.
5. What is the basis of content organization of most instrumental method books and how does this influence instruction?
6. What are some of the more recent developments that have con-tributed to the continued growth of school instrumental music?
7. What are some important considerations when recruiting begin-ning instrumentalists?
8. How have research efforts affected school instrumental music teaching?
9. Considering the past 150 years, what do you foresee as the future of school instrumental music instruction?

References

BENNER, CHARLES H. (1972). *Teaching performing groups.* Washington, D.C.: Music Educators National Conference.

BIRGE, EDWARD BAILEY. ([1928, 1939] 1966). *History of public school music in the United States,* new and augmented edition. Washington, D.C.: Music Educators National Conference.

BROWN, JOSEPH D. (1985). *School band recruitment and dropout issues.* Elkhart, IN: Gemeinhardt Co., Inc.

BRYANT, CAROL. (1975). *And the band played on.* Washington, D.C.: Smithsonian Institution Press.

Dance, music, theatre, visual arts: National standards for arts education. (1994). Reston, VA: Music Educators National Conference.

DUERKSEN, GEORGE L. (1972). *Teaching instrumental music.* Washington, D.C.: Music Educators National Conference.

DEVERICH, ROBIN K. (1987). The Maidstone movement—influential British precursor of American public school instrumental classes. *Journal of Research in Music Education* 35 (1), 39–55.

ELLIOTT, DAVID J. (1995). *Music matters.* New York: Oxford University Press.

FLEMING, LISSA A. (1994). *Getting started with jazz band.* Reston, VA: Music Educators National Conference.

FROSETH, JAMES O. (1970). *The individualized instructor.* Chicago: GIA Publications, Inc.

———. (1971). Using MAP scores in the instruction of beginning students in instrumental music. *Journal of Research in Music Education* 19 (1), 98–105.

———. (1974). *NABIM recruiting manual.* Chicago: GIA Publications, Inc.

———. (1982). *The comprehensive music instructor: listen, move, sing and play.* Chicago: GIA Publications, Inc.

GAROFALO, ROBERT J. (1983a). *Blueprint for band.* Fort Lauderdale, FL: Meredith Music Publications.

———. (1983b). *Rehearsal handbook for band and orchestra students.* Fort Lauderdale, FL: Meredith Music Publications.

GORDON, EDWIN E. ([1965] 1988). *Musical aptitude profile.* Chicago: Riverside Publishing Co.

———. (1982). *Intermediate measures of music audiation.* Chicago: GIA Publications Inc.

———. (1984). *Instrument timbre preference test.* Chicago: GIA Publications Inc.

Guidelines for performances of school music groups: Expectations and limitations. (1986). Reston, VA: Music Educators National Conference.

KINNEY, GUY. (1981). *Complete guide to teaching small instrumental groups in the high school.* West Nyack, NY: Parker Publishing Co.

KLINEDINST, RICHARD E. (1991). Predicting performance achievement and retention of fifth-grade instrumental students. *Journal of Research in Music Education* 39 (3), 225–238.

———. (1992). Predicting performance achievement of beginning band students—second year results. *Contributions to Music Education* 19, 46–59.

MADDY, JOSEPH, and THADDEUS GIDDINGS. (1923, 1926). *The universal teacher.* Elkhart, IN: C. G. Conn; Cincinnati: The Willis Music Co.

MAYER, FREDERICK R., ed. (1993). *The string orchestra super list.* Reston, VA: Music Educators National Conference.

MERRIMAN, LYLE C. (1978). *Woodwind research guide.* Evanston, IL: The Instrumentalist Co.
MITCHELL, ALBERT. (1924). *Class method for violin.* Boston: Oliver Ditson Co.
Musical Truth 9. (1917). Elkhart, IN: C. G. Conn.
NORMANN, THEODORE. (1941). *Instrumental music in the public schools.* Philadelphia: Oliver Ditson Co.
PAYNTER, JOHN P. (1977). *The community band.* Deerfield, IL: Northshore Concert Band & NABIM.
PETERS, CHARLES, and MATT BETTON. (1972). *Take one.* Park Ridge, IL: Neil A. Kjos Music Co.
REUL, DAVID G. (1994). *Getting started with middle level band.* Reston, VA: Music Educators National Conference.
ROHNER, JAMES M. (1995). 1995 survey of school music budgets. *The Instrumentalist* 50 (2), 19–28.
ROTH, RAYMOND. (1981). Don't they also love music? *The Instrumentalist* 36 (5), 102–103, 110.
Rubank elementary method. (1934). Chicago: Rubank, Inc.
SCHMID, WILL. (1992). World music in the instrumental program. *Music Educators Journal* 78 (9), 41–45.
Selmer music guidance survey. n.d. Elkhart, IN: The Selmer Co.
SOLLINGER, CHARLES EDMOND. (1970). The musical men and the professors—A history of string class methods in the U.S., 1800–1911. Ph.D. diss., University of Michigan; cited in James A. Keene. (1982). *A history of music education in the United States.* Hanover, NH: University Press of New England.
STUBER, BENJAMIN. (1923). *Instrumental music course.* Chicago: E. T. Root & Sons.
SUZUKI, SHINICHI. (1969). *Nurtured by love,* trans. Waltraud Suzuki. New York: Exposition Press.
Teaching stringed instruments: A course of study. (1991a). Reston, VA: Music Educators National Conference.
Teaching wind and percussion instruments: A course of study. (1991b). Reston, VA: Music Educators National Conference.
VOLK, TERESE M. (1993). The history and development of multicultural music education as evidenced in the *Music Educators Journal,* 1967–1992. *Journal of Research in Music Education* 41 (2), 137–155.
ZERULL, DAVID S. (1994). *Getting started with high school band.* Reston, VA: Music Educators National Conference.

For Further Reading

FENNELL, FREDERICK. (1954). *Time and the winds.* Kenosha, WI: Leblanc Publications, Inc.
GREEN, ELIZABETH. (1966). *Teaching stringed instruments in classes.* Englewood Cliffs, NJ: Prentice-Hall, Inc.
HAZEN, MARGARET HINELLE, and ROBERT M. HAZEN. (1987). *The music men: An illustrated history of brass bands in America, 1800–1920.* Washington, D.C.: Smithsonian Institution Press.

HOLZ, EMIL A., and ROGER E. JACOBI. (1966). *Teaching band instruments to beginners.* Englewood Cliffs, NJ: Prentice-Hall, Inc.

HUMPHREYS, JERE T. (1989). An overview of American public school bands and orchestras before World War II. *Bulletin of the Council for Research in Music Education* 101, 50–60.

KEENE, JAMES A. (1982). *A history of music education in the United States.* Hanover, NH: University Press of New England.

MARK, MICHAEL L., and CHARLES L. GARY. (1992). *A history of American music education.* New York: Schirmer Books.

PRESCOTT, GERALD R., and LAWRENCE W. CHIDESTER. (1938). *Getting results with school bands.* New York: Carl Fischer, Inc.; Minneapolis: Paul A. Schmitt Music Co.

The Process of Learning Music

American music educators traditionally have been advocates of getting things done, be it vocal and instrumental instruction or just philosophizing about the objectives of music education. They have not, however, been equally alert to possible improvements in music instruction suggested by the findings of research in the psychology of learning. To an extent, the upshot of this situation has been an unintentional neglect of both important factual data and learning theory in favor of more or less traditional methods of instruction. As a consequence, the instructional program in many instances has lacked the direction which learning theory can provide. Theory and practice have not always been in agreement.

In the thirty-eight years since Louis P. Thorpe (1958, p. 163) made this observation, much has been learned and published about the process of learning. The application of this knowledge to music learning is only the beginning. Most instrumental music teachers teach the way they were taught as children; they seldom examine or question traditional methods and techniques of instruction with regard to current theories and knowledge about music learning. Good, bad, and inefficient methods and techniques of teaching music persist through unquestioned adherence to tradition.

How music is learned and how it should be taught has been the subject of scrutiny by some music educators and learning theorists. Most of what is written is personal opinion based on experiences in teaching music. Some is based on general psychological principles applied to music learning. Only a small amount is based on experimental research. Perhaps the overriding cause for inefficient music teaching is music teachers who lack skills in diagnosing and prescribing musical and instrumental problems. Instead of diagnostic proficiency we find perpetual trial and error. By forgetting and/or ignoring what are known to be efficient techniques for teaching instrumental music, teachers often substitute reliance on materials in the order printed in "method" books. Music instruction under such circumstances becomes simply a series of favorite techniques that keep students occupied, working, and sometimes learning.

Rather than attempting to relate a history of learning theories, the discussion in this chapter will center around contributions of selected psychologists, music educators, and researchers who have provided important ideas for improving music teaching and learning. Those chosen for inclusion are well known for their impact on education. It is interesting to note the degree of commonality among their theories and how the theories relate to the practice of teaching music.

Of course, it is beyond the scope of this book to cover the entire field of learning processes. Selected references for further reading and study are included at the end of the chapter.

Educators, Psychologists, and Music Learning

Johann Heinrich Pestalozzi (1746–1827) was a Swiss educator whose ideas and practices have had considerable influence on general education and school music teaching in this country. He believed the purpose of education was the development of the whole person rather than the mastery of individual skills; integrating the moral, physical, and mental faculties produced a well-rounded individual. Learning was facilitated by the inductive method, which includes three steps: 1) Concepts must be taught by experiencing whole objects, pictures, or things before names or symbols are associated. Learning occurs by moving from the known to the unknown. 2) After experiencing the whole, its parts are analyzed and then labeled. 3) The parts of the whole are synthesized, and the concept is considered as an abstract. Pestalozzi's ideas first became popular in Europe and then spread to this country in the early 1800s. Although Pestalozzi never taught music, his ideas were applied to music teaching by European educators at the time. Lowell Mason is credited with adapting much of the process to teaching music reading in Boston during the 1830s. Various adaptations of Mason's techniques continued to the end of the nineteenth century.

A psychologist who influenced many music teachers during the first half of this century was James L. Mursell (1893–1963). For over thirty years his writings covered topics of school music objectives, curriculum, implementation techniques, measurement, and the psychology of music. Mursell and Mabelle Glenn wrote *The Psychology of School Music Teaching* in 1931 "to bring together all the findings of psychological research which bear on the work of the school music teacher, and to show how they can help in dealing with the practical problems to be faced" (p. 1). Many of the points made in the book have remained valid through the years, while other points are now outmoded by clearer understandings of learning processes.

Three of Mursell's basic tenets that remain current and valid are: 1) technique should be an outgrowth of musical expression, 2) familiarity with musical sounds should precede music reading, and 3) music should be taught in a cyclical sequence. These three principles are particularly appropriate to teaching instrumental music.

Mursell built a strong case for teaching musical skills and techniques through the demands of music. He was determined that musical expression should be the goal for technique development. Technical skills should be a means to an end rather than the goal itself; musicianship should be of primary importance.

Mursell also advocated the necessity for teaching music-reading, so that students could understand and manipulate musical concepts. Learning to read music should be the result of immediate musical experiences. "They [symbols] must be taught always in terms of their musical meanings and in application to musical situations and experiences, never merely in terms of verbal definitions and arithmetical designations" (Mursell, 1958, p. 153). This approach is directly related to Pestalozzi's thinking that concepts should be experienced before labels and symbols are applied.

Based on his understanding of human growth and development, Mursell, in his later years, proposed that music content should be taught in a cyclical sequence. "In a cyclical sequence, the various items that need to be presented do not occur once for all at some predetermined time. They appear again and again, always in new settings, always with added meanings" (Mursell, 1958, p. 157). Take, for example, the introduction of levels of dynamics in instrumental performance where initial attention is directed to loud and soft levels. Over a period of years of continued training, meaning and understanding of dynamics expand with increased performance skills and awareness to stylistic and expressive performance. This conceptualization of learning has been supported by other psychologists and has influenced many school curricula. The application of cyclical process to teaching music is appropriate; however, a problem still exists when the sequence of music content has not been efficiently or logically determined.

The thinking and writings of Jerome S. Bruner have had considerable impact on public school education processes during the past three decades. In *The Process of Education*, Bruner (1960) develops four main topics: 1) the role of structure in learning, 2) readiness for learning, 3) the nature of intuition, and 4) motivation to learn. His discussions are not specific to teaching any particular subject and may be generalized to music teaching. Bruner states that "the curriculum of a subject should be determined by the most fundamental understanding that can be achieved of the underlying principles that give structure to that subject" (p. 31). Comprehension and recall are possible when fundamentals are understood and details are presented within structured patterns. For example, applying this in a music context, students who have gradually acquired a vocabulary of tonal and rhythm patterns are then able to take music dictation of melodies by recognizing familiar patterns within a melodic exercise. As subject matter is structured and comprehended, transfer of learning to unfamiliar situations also becomes possible.

Bruner explains his concept of readiness as "the proposition that the foundations of any subject may be taught to anybody at any age in some form" (1960, p. 12). This means that children of differing age levels and adults could learn the fundamentals of music if the fundamentals are presented in an appropriate form. Bruner supports the contention that children pass through various stages of intellectual development, and that learning tasks and content should be appropriate for whatever their level. He also declares that learning a subject involves three processes—acquisition of new material, transformation of knowledge to fit unfamiliar circumstances, and evaluation of the appropriateness of the transformation. A series of episodes, each including the three processes, builds a knowledge of subject matter.

The term *spiral curriculum* is used by Bruner to explain how fundamentals of a subject matter gradually expand in depth and complexity as the learner proceeds through various grade levels and continues to study and apply the same concepts. This is similar to Mursell's cyclical sequence. In order for the concept of readiness to be operational in a music curriculum, it would be essential for the content and the learning process to be carefully sequenced with continuity through all grade levels.

Bruner advocates that education should include the training of intuitive thinking; intuition, he explains, involves immediate apprehension of a "whole." In music, intuitive thinking could be fostered through such activities as composing, arranging, and improvising. This process of arriving at conclusions without prior analysis is not emphasized in much of our current music teaching.

Bruner's final point is that the willingness or motivation to learn is most effective when based on what is to be accomplished. For example, when students enjoy performing music on an instrument and expressing themselves musically, they are more motivated to continue receiving instruction and to practice performance skills.

In *Toward a Theory of Instruction*, Bruner (1966) states that a theory of instruction for a subject must be prescriptive and normative. An instructional theory must be based on effective experiences, efficient structure of knowledge, sequence of content, and pacing of rewards for learning. All of these concerns are a necessary part of teaching instrumental music. Experience through activities is the basis for content sequence. Sequencing musical content is of particular interest in the succeeding chapters of this book. Bruner (1966, p. 49) states:

> Instruction consists of leading the learner through a sequence of
> statements and restatements of a problem or body of knowledge
> that increases the learner's ability to grasp, transform, and transfer
> what he is learning. In short, the sequence in which a learner
> encounters materials within a domain of knowledge affects the difficulty he will have in achieving mastery.

The psychologist Robert M. Gagné ([1965] 1977) influenced music educators with his hierarchy of "conditions" or levels of learning. Gagné divided the learning process into four basic perceptual levels—Signal Learning, Stimulus-Response Learning, Chaining, and Verbal Association; and four basic conceptual levels—Multiple-Discrimination Learning, Concept Learning, Principle Learning, and Problem Solving. Gagné's learning conditions provide a structure for sequencing learning processes and subject content. The levels of learning are a series of prerequisites for understanding the concepts that comprise subject matter. Edwin Gordon (1971) first discussed the application of Gagné's classifications of learning to music education. Later, Robert Sidnell (1973) provided music content examples for each of the eight levels. Most recently, Campbell and Scott-Kassner (1995, p. 34) provide applications of Gagné's theory to music for children.

Benjamin S. Bloom (1985) and his associates completed an extensive study (Development of Talent Research Project) of over 120 individuals who exhibited the highest levels of accomplishment in the arts, cognitive fields, or athletics before reaching age thirty-five. The study was intended to provide information about how we learn and how we fulfill our potentials. The subjects were swimmers, sculptors, mathematicians, scientists, tennis champions, and a group of highly accomplished young concert pianists. Bloom and Sosniak (1981) compared talent development and school experiences and stated, "In general, school learning emphasizes group learning and the subject or skills to be learned. Talent development typically emphasizes the individual and his or her progress in a particular activity" (p. 90). They further pointed out the role of home support in learning: "In general, where the school teaches the same subject or skill that parents emphasize, learning is likely to be very great—unless there are conflicts between the home and the teacher about the way to teach it."

Other generalizations from the Bloom study are that support, attention, and rewards from teachers and family were critical at all points for development of talented individuals; all subjects of the study began instruction at an early age and took at least ten years of work to reach high levels of accomplishment; learning and instruction progressed in phases, with each phase a prerequisite to the next. All of those studied were dedicated, hard workers. Bloom also mentioned that the children spent as much time on their talent development as other children spend in television viewing. Four general qualities that appeared across the six talent fields were 1) a strong interest in and emotional commitment to a particular talent field; 2) the desire to reach a high level of attainment in the talent field; 3) the willingness to put in the great amounts of time and effort needed to reach very high levels of achievement in the talent field; and 4) the ability to learn rapidly and well, especially by middle stages of development. Mastering early prerequisites has a positive effect on the quality and rate of learning.

It can be generalized from Bloom's results that the musical talents of all levels of students will be furthered by school music teachers who ana-lyze their own teaching procedures and content and improve their teaching skills. Parent support for beginning instrumentalists is necessary for early and continued success. The importance of knowing how to learn and how to teach music effectively should not be underestimated.

The research and writings of Howard Gardner (1983, 1985, 1991, 1993) are having an impact in music education recently. Gardner is perhaps best known for his theory of multiple intelligences, in which he postulates that we have a variety and mix of possible intelligences that are basically discrete. He currently identifies seven areas: linguis-tic, logical-mathematical, spatial, bodily-kinesthetic, interpersonal, intrapersonal, and musical. Note that these areas go beyond the tradi-tional language and mathematics emphases in "intelligence" tests. As does Bruner, Gardner advocates training intuitive thinking along with scholarly learning and skills. Learners move to levels of understanding through gaining facility with language and symbol systems and through problem solving within meaningful contexts.

The role of schools, according to Gardner, is to develop the intelli-gences of individual students to their highest potential and help guide students into vocations where they will be successful and constructive. To accommodate the various ways that children learn requires teachers who are flexible in approaches to presentation and techniques. Recognizing the existence of a separate musical intelligence has profound implica-tions for music teachers and learners, including justifying music training for all schoolchildren. We are only beginning to systematically examine the music-learning process, and useful information is emerging.

Generalizing from Psychology to Music

Through the years, efforts have been made by a few music teachers to apply the thinking of psychologists and educators to music instruction.

One of the earliest examples is the influence of the Swiss educator Pestalozzi's ideas on Lowell Mason. Mason adapted many Pestalozzian principles to music education in Boston during the 1830s and urged teachers

> 1. To teach sounds before signs and to make the child learn to sing before he learns the written notes or their names;
> 2. To lead him to observe by hearing and imitating sounds, their resemblances and differences, their agreeable and disagreeable effect, instead of explaining these things to him—in a word, to make active instead of passive in learning;
> 3. To teach but one thing at a time—rhythm, melody, and expression to be taught and practiced separately, before the child is called to the difficult task of attending to all at once;
> 4. To make him practice each step of each of these divisions, until he is master of it, before passing to the next;
> 5. To give the principles and theory after the practice, and as induction from it;
> 6. To analyze and practice the elements of articulate sound in order to apply them to music; and
> 7. To have the names of the notes correspond to those used in instrumental music. (Monroe, 1907, p. 145)

Mason put into practice a whole-part-whole method for learning to read music through singing. Music was experienced by singing and then analyzed, read, and conceptualized.

More recently, Emil A. Holz and Roger E. Jacobi (1966, pp. 46–50) listed five basic principles of instrumental class instruction. The principles are of interest because they directly reflect Mason's applications of Pestalozzian principles and are quoted here with some abbreviation:

> 1. . . . learning is often most effective when experience precedes theory, or in Pestalozzian terms, the thing before the sign.
> 2. . . . the teacher must organize instruction in such a way as to proceed from the known to the unknown.
> 3. The learning process proceeds most effectively when it is organized in such a way that the specific is related to the general and the general to the specific—in other words, from the whole to the parts and back again.

4. Throughout the educational process the teacher must realize
that the important activity in the classroom is not teaching but
learning, and that learning depends upon the desire to learn.
5. . . . teaching is the art of making students want to learn. In the
beginning instrumental music class, then, teaching is not conducting, not lecturing, not judging. Teaching is motivating, explaining,
demonstrating, encouraging, suggesting, organizing, and evaluating.

The field of psychology has provided many insights into the general
learning process, and much may be generalized to music learning.
Research by psychologists has resulted in many areas of consensus
about how learning occurs. It is generally accepted that the learning
process is much more complex than early researchers believed. Moving
from the known to the unknown is a basic tenet, but a sequence of prerequisites appears to exist within both the "known" and "unknown"
stages.

Some examples of conclusions we can make from the works of the
theorists discussed and others are most useful to music learning and
are listed in Table 2.1.

Many of the topics listed in the table will be expanded on later in
this book. More and more music educators are beginning to pay closer
attention to research in psychology and music. Selected psychologists
and music educators have participated in various symposia and conferences, such as the three Ann Arbor Symposia held at the University
of Michigan between 1978 and 1982 and the Biology of Music Making
Conferences held in Denver in 1984 and 1987. The Crane Symposium
held at the State University of New York at Potsdam in 1986 is of particular interest in that its theme was "Toward an Understanding of the
Teaching and Learning of Music Performance." Detailed teaching suggestions from the Crane Symposium will appear in later chapters of
this book.

Sequencing Music Instruction

In traditional instrumental music instruction, a basic assumption is
that repetition is of prime importance: the more repetition, the more
learning and retention. Teaching students "how to practice" often
means training them to discover and repeat problem spots until errors

Table 2.1

EXAMPLES OF RESEARCH APPLICATIONS
TO TEACHING MUSIC

Memory functions with short-term and long-term effects and involves the encoding and retrieval of information through organizing, classifying, and manipulating. Learning a vocabulary of rhythm and tonal patterns through labeling the sounds facilitates remembering music and becoming functional with composition and improvisation.

Frequent review is probably more efficient than drills for reinforcing new concepts and skills. Building on previously learned musical skills is enhanced by review activities that keep earlier learning current and usable.

Complex tasks are learned by properly sequencing the content and following the prerequisite steps. Much less is known about prerequisites in music learning when compared to what is known and practiced in the teaching of mathematics or reading. Teaching and learning gain efficiency when prerequisites are carefully sequenced.

Tasks must be of appropriate difficulty to avoid undue frustration or loss of interest. This is particularly important when teaching music to young instrumentalists.

Diagnostic and prescriptive teaching is possible when effective content and learning sequences are followed. This is a key factor in meeting needs of individual learners and for becoming an efficient, effective teacher.

It is possible to make the teacher dispensable by learning how to learn. A primary goal of teaching should be to help students become self-sufficient learners.

Active participation improves chances for learning to occur. Learning music is enhanced through demonstrating musical performance skills.

Learning is easier when the content is put to immediate use. Success in learning facilitates further success.

are somehow corrected. Little attention has been given to the development of efficient sequences of musical content and learning processes with instrumental teaching. It is essential to go beyond simple imitation and rote learning in instrumental teaching and emphasize musical meaning and understanding.

Meyer (1989) organizes musical qualities into syntactic parameters (pitch patterns and rhythm patterns) and nonsyntactic parameters (timbre, texture, tempo, articulation, and dynamics). Syntactic parameters differ from nonsyntactic parameters in that they have a proportionality that may occur in organized patterns. Patterns of pitch and rhythm are important building blocks for perceiving, learning, and understanding music.

Gordon (1993) has developed a sequence for learning music through tonal and rhythmic patterns. Based on Gagné's conditions of learning and also related to Pestalozzian principles, the Gordon music-learning sequence has five levels of discrimination (perceptual) learning: Aural/Oral, Verbal Association, Partial Synthesis, Symbolic Association, and Composite Synthesis; and three levels of inference (conceptual) learning: Generalization, Creativity/Improvisation, and Theoretical Understanding.

Discrimination levels are mainly concerned with the taking in of information, or *perceiving*, and the development of a vocabulary that facilitates audiation. Discrimination learning occurs with the familiar and known. Inference levels are concerned with the transfer and manipulation of patterns and information, or *conceiving*. Inference occurs when working with the unfamiliar and unknown. A musical vocabulary of tonal and rhythm patterns is acquired through the sequence and may then be performed instrumentally. Three important points to keep in mind as pattern content progresses through the learning skills sequence are: 1) Is music notation present during instruction or not? 2) Is the tonal or rhythm pattern familiar or unfamiliar? 3) Is it extracted from a familiar or unfamiliar tune?

Each of the levels of Gordon's learning-skills sequence is summarized along with specific teaching examples as follows:

Aural/Oral (A/O) is level one of discrimination learning and refers to rote learning of tones through singing or playing an instrument, and of rhythm through experiencing body-movement responses to music. Tonal patterns are learned without rhythm interaction, and rhythm patterns are learned without tonal interaction. Listening to music and imitating the sounds of tonal and rhythmic patterns are basic to beginning music learning and require minimal "musical thinking," but the result is aural familiarity with patterns of musical sounds. Example: Teacher sings a tonal pattern on "loo" and student echo-sings.

Verbal Association (VA) consists of the attachment of syllable labels (such as movable *do*) to patterns of sound after much A/O activity occurs. Word labels are also used for classifications and categories, such as *major*, *minor*, *duple*, and *triple*. The verbal encoding of tonal and rhythmic pattern sounds with syllables begins without music notation and facilitates their classification, memory, retrieval, and synthesis. Example: Teacher sings a tonal pattern using movable *do* syllables and student echo-sings. Students are ready to move to the next level when they are given the sound of a familiar tonal or rhythm pattern, and they can accurately provide the syllables with the sounds.

Partial Synthesis (PS) is the beginning of musical syntax through aural combinations of patterns or recognizing learned patterns in familiar music without notation. Synthesis involves the connecting of familiar vocabulary patterns into familiar larger structures. It also involves developing aural recognition of tonality and meter of familiar music. Example: Teacher asks, "How many songs do you know that begin with *do re mi?*

Symbolic Association (SA) involves visually attaching music notation to familiar pattern vocabulary. This must involve both reading and writing music symbols after the previous levels of discrimination are accomplished for any given vocabulary pattern. Example: Teacher provides students with notation as a "picture" of a pattern which they can aurally identify by sound with tonal syllables.

Composite Synthesis (CS) is the development of music syntax through visually recognizing familiar patterns and phrases in notation of familiar music. Recognition involves audiating the sounds of the music notation when reading or writing familiar patterns. Example: Teacher prompts, "Look at the music and count how many times *do re mi* occurs."

Generalization (G) is the first level of inference learning and requires using familiar vocabulary to comprehend the unfamiliar; it is thus the moving from the known to the unknown. Generalization occurs when familiar vocabulary patterns are recognized in unfamiliar music both with or without notation present. It also occurs when students can correctly add syllables to unfamiliar patterns. Generalization may occur at A/O, VA, or SA levels. Sight-reading is Generalization at the SA level. Example: Teacher says, "Listen to this unfamiliar song and raise your hand when you hear *do re mi.*"

Creativity/Improvisation (C/I) occurs when familiar vocabulary is manipulated to improvise, arrange, or compose variations or new compositions. It is possible to spiral to Creativity/Improvisation from the A/O and SA levels. Example: Teacher assigns an eight-measure composition that must include the pattern *do re mi.*

Theoretical Understanding (TU) includes explanations of why things occur as they do in music; for example, intervallic relationships, scale construction, and note proportionalities. Music theory is analogous to grammar and parts of speech in language. Music theory is often confused by music teachers with the symbols and labels used in music notation. Theoretical Understanding may occur at A/O, VA, and SA levels. Theoretical information is of little functional use until music content has moved through all previous levels of the sequence and audiation skills develop. Example: Teacher asks, "What is the interval between *do* and *mi*?"

A unique feature of the preceding sequence is the Verbal Association level. All of the levels of Gordon's learning sequence are essential components, but Verbal Association may be the crux of the sequence. Tonal and rhythm syllables are first associated aurally with sounds of specific patterns rather than with the notation of patterns. The syllables, in effect, become the "words" for remembering and manipulating familiar patterns before notation is introduced. Syllable systems have been used by music teachers for many years but in nearly all cases have been initially associated with music notation rather than sound.

Most instrumental teachers ignore teaching verbal associations of tonal patterns altogether and shortcut the process by beginning students with notation associated with fingerings to produce approximate pitches. A variety of rhythm syllables are widely subscribed to, but their purpose is almost always to associate first with rhythm notation rather than rhythmic feeling of patterns. A typical example of a sequence problem is introducing a counting system in symbols concurrently with music notation.

Some instrumental music teachers have students first listen to the sounds and then move directly to notation. Although a necessary prerequisite to music reading, informal music listening in itself is inadequate without a Verbal Association stage. The purpose of Verbal Association needs to be the labeling of musical *sounds*, not symbols. Just as we acquire a language vocabulary of words that allows us to think and communicate, we acquire and label a vocabulary of tonal and rhythm sounds that facilitates our ability to think and communicate musically.

The Gordon music-learning sequence facilitates diagnostic and prescriptive teaching. The level of students' music achievement may be

Table 2.2

SUMMARY OF LEVELS AND SUBLEVELS
OF SKILL-LEARNING SEQUENCE

DISCRIMINATION LEARNING

    Aural/Oral (A/O)

    Verbal Association (VA)

    Partial Synthesis (PS)

    Symbolic Association (SA)

        Reading—Writing

    Composite Synthesis (CS)

        Reading—Writing

INFERENCE LEARNING

    Generalization (G)

        Aural/Oral—Verbal—Symbolic [Reading—Writing]

    Creativity/Improvisation (C/I)

        Aural/Oral—Symbolic [Reading—Writing]

    Theoretical Understanding (TU)

        Aural/Oral—Verbal—Symbolic [Reading—Writing]

From Gordon, 1993, p. 55.

assessed and the next step prescribed according to sequences for learning and content. Learners should progress cumulatively through the five discrimination and three inference levels in sequence, with the occasional exception of spiraling activities as indicated above in the inference level descriptions. If a student is unable to read certain patterns in notation, it would be appropriate to return to more instruction at the A/O, VA, and PS levels before proceeding again with reading activities. Prerequisites of discrimination levels must be accomplished before inference tasks of Generalization, Creativity/Improvisation, and Theoretical Understanding become meaningful and appropriate. Students should have frequent opportunities for inference learning, as new vocabulary is acquired in discrimination levels.

The sequence of skills for learning music is basically the same regardless of the age of the learner. The main difference in working with young children compared to older children or adults is the pacing and choice of materials and techniques. Younger children generally need more time with Aural/Oral activities. Older children and adults may often move more rapidly into music notation and are more analytical and comfortable with working with symbols as beginning music learners.

Gordon coined the term *audiation* to label the phenomena of hearing and comprehending musical sounds whether or not the actual sounds or notation are present. He maintains that "audiation is the basis of music aptitude and music achievement. As a consequence, it is also the basis of music learning theory. . . . Audiation is to music what thought is to speech" (Gordon, 1993, p. 13). Gordon proposes that audiation is the basis for music achievement and aptitude and that there are eight types and six stages of audiation. Readers are urged to examine Chapters 2–4 of *Learning Sequences in Music* (Gordon, 1993) for complete explanations of his theories. In effect, when we perform on a musical instrument we should audiate *before* the instrument sounds occur. We then have an internal model of the desired sounds to compare with the instrumental results. A primary focus of teaching instrumentalists is to first build their audiation skills. Using learning skills and content sequences facilitates that objective.

Language and Music Learning

A useful analogy to learning sequence in music is the sequence of events by which we acquire language facility as children. Learning to read and comprehend language has many corollaries to learning to read and comprehend music. It should be noted, however, that research does not support similarities in brain activity in language and music acquisition. Nevertheless, the overt parallels are obvious. Acquiring verbal skills is dependent mainly on the ability to hear and discriminate sounds and then attach meaning to them. Acquiring musical skill and understanding is also dependent mainly on the ability to hear and discriminate sounds and attach meaning to them.

If every paragraph you read first had to be rote-taught to you, you would be a very inefficient reader. You not only would read a minimum of material, but you would gain little or no meaning from the symbols. In addition, you would have great difficulty transferring your reading skills to unfamiliar materials. We do not expect children to learn to speak without first hearing speech. In addition, children gain vocabulary and verbal facility over a long time period through speech alone and without a symbol system.

Children learn to talk and later read through first hearing language. Initial attempts to vocalize are called babble. Eventually, they begin verbal expression and communication by imitating sounds of simple words for familiar objects (e.g., milk, food, cup, foot, hand, etc.) or for actions (e.g., run, walk, play, hold, see, etc.). Syntax and meaning are gradually developed through chaining words together into phrases and sentences. Initial language efforts are often used for expressing needs and feelings (e.g., Want drink!). The first few years of life include developing a fairly large vocabulary of spoken words. Initial reading efforts involve seeing symbols for familiar spoken words and associating sounds and meanings. It is highly recommended that when beginning to read, learners hear words read to them by others. It is also important for beginning readers to learn to write familiar spoken words. Writing compositions with familiar vocabulary is also encouraged. Spoken vocabulary continues to expand as reading skills develop. Gradually, reading independence is gained for the vocabulary of words known (heard and understood), and then the ability to generalize to the unfamiliar is possible. Spoken vocabulary is larger than reading or writing vocabulary during the initial years of learning to read; later, reading vocabulary surpasses spoken vocabulary. Lastly, children learn the theory of language, e.g., grammar, parts of speech, and sentence structure.

Music learning follows the same basic sequence of events for language learning. Gordon's learning skills sequence parallels this in large part. Music must first be heard and experienced (A/O) over a long time period. Aural familiarity is gained with listening to and experiencing simple melodies, rhythms, and patterns. Imitating pitch and rhythm patterns (babbling) and eventually singing simple songs is our initial attempt to "speak" music and develop repertoire (vocabulary). Tonal and rhythmic patterns should gradually receive syllable associations without notation and become meaningful entities (VA, PS).

Symbols (notation) are then systematically introduced to represent familiar patterns (SA, CS). Reading and writing activities are appropriate at this point and should be encouraged. Unfamiliar music may then be learned and manipulated on the basis of what is known and familiar (G, C/I). Finally, it is appropriate to introduce the theoretical aspects of music, e.g., intervals, voice leading, and chord writing (TU). Throughout, audiation skills are developing and refining.

Application of language models of learning to instrumental music instruction has been of interest to jazz educators because jazz performance demands improvisation facility, and improvisation skills may be developed through first acquiring a vocabulary of tonal and rhythm patterns. The following is an aural-imitative method suggested for jazz pedagogy by Barry L. Velleman (1978, pp. 28–31), a linguist:

Ear training should precede music reading, and music reading should precede transcription

Class time should be used primarily for drilling improvisational patterns, usually without reference to written materials

Assignments should consist of the memorization of solo passages in addition to the preparation of class exercises.

Explanation and theorization should be given less importance than the actual playing of patterns.

As the lessons proceed, the instructor's cues should become less specific and contain progressively fewer elements of the desired student response.

Velleman also emphasizes the necessity for students to model patterns of sounds after hearing the instructor. Terminology (VA) is then initially associated with the sounds (A/O) rather than the symbols (SA).

Learning and Instrumental Music

Instrumental music could be taught exclusively through rote training of songs and melodies. Many jazz and popular music performers, for example, do not read music. However, instrumental performers who do read music have a vast amount of solo and ensemble music literature available to them. It is much more efficient to perform on instruments when music-reading skills are developed. A primary purpose for development of efficient music-learning sequences is to produce functional musicians with music-reading skills. This does not mean, however, that instrumentalists should be able to perform only from notation. Playing "by ear" and improvising should be a continuing part of performance practice, especially for those who are proficient music readers. After all, we still talk after learning to read.

It is assumed that beginning instrumentalists in school music programs should read music. Unfortunately, most students do not read music when beginning on an instrument, so they are given the instrument and a music book and are expected to learn music reading concurrently with the instrument. This is somewhat like learning to read as you learn to talk. Music readiness must occur first so that students have something to express with their instruments. Only then does notation take on musical connotations.

Teachers should emphasize that an instrument and the voice are merely means for students to demonstrate and express what they know musically. When beginning instrumentalists do not have prerequisite music-reading skills, it is best to begin by singing and performing without written music. Consider how accomplished jazz performers who do not read music notation develop their instrumental skills. Technique of the instrument is acquired to express musical ideas, not learned for its own sake with a forced application of musical expression added later. An excellent source of tunes is familiar songs from general music classes and folk music from many cultures.

Some instrumental music instructors speak negatively about rote training and believe that students fail to learn music reading when rote taught. These instructors do not understand or recognize the importance of initial rote training of songs and pattern vocabularies and the process of verbal association which then leads to music reading. Audiation is dependent on A/O and VA experiences.

Many problems occur in instrumental music instruction because of the common practice of beginning with the symbols rather than the sounds and omitting enough aural/oral practice and efficient verbal association of patterns. Students are mainly expected to learn the technical skills of instruments while associating fingerings with music notation. By skipping the musical readiness for notation, music symbols become visual cues for fingerings rather than for musical sounds.

Instrument performance becomes analogous to typewriting series of words without understanding the language.

McPherson (1993, p. 331), in a landmark study of instrumental students in Australian high schools, proposes five essential performance skills for success on a musical instrument—playing by ear, sight-reading, playing from memory, performing rehearsed music proficiently, and improvising. He maintains that playing by ear is the most fundamental skill. Using path analysis, he found that playing by ear relates highly to improvisation skills and influence sight-reading skill. Sight-reading relates highly to performing rehearsed music proficiently. Both playing by ear and sight-reading influence playing from memory. McPherson also points out that "students exposed to a traditional, visually oriented approach to learning a musical instrument are typically inefficient in their ability to audiate music from notation or aurally. These results show the extent to which a visually oriented system of training fails to develop the important capacity to 'think in sound,' which is essential to all musical performance" (p. 327). The results of his study support the existence, interrelatedness, and need of the five components, and he recommends a balanced approach to instruction that includes all five.

Much remains to be ascertained about how music is learned. It is quite possible that more than one efficient learning sequence may exist. The level of learners' music aptitude may interact with various sequences of content or learning. High-aptitude students may learn somewhat differently from low-aptitude students. Individual differences may be accommodated in various ways. Without a doubt, learning music and performing musically on instruments are complex tasks.

The following three chapters are concerned with the application of learning sequence to instrumental music teaching. Tonal and rhythmic content and teaching techniques are approached through logical sequences. Instrumental technique is accomplished through musical content. All of the psychologists and educators discussed in this chapter have contributed to the approaches used; however, much of the structure and terminology is influenced by the writings of Edwin Gordon. In addition, the knowledgeable reader will recognize many of the same teaching techniques popularized in music-education approaches by Shinichi Suzuki, Carl Orff, Emile-Jaques Dalcroze, and Zoltan Kodály. A basic difference is the systematic and sequential application of the teaching techniques within a learning-sequence structure. The materials and techniques that are advocated have been successfully field-tested by the author and many of his students.

Review Questions

1. What is a major cause of ineffective instrumental music teaching?
2. How did Pestalozzi's ideas influence music teaching?
3. What basic tenets of Mursell are especially applicable to instrumental music teaching?
4. What is Bruner's concept of "readiness"?
5. How does Mursell's cyclical sequence compare with Bruner's spiral curriculum?
6. What are the implications of the results from Bloom's Development of Talent Project for teaching instrumental music?
7. What are some of the implications for music teaching when we recognize that musical intelligence exists as one of our human intelligences?
8. What are some of the current areas of consensus about how learning occurs?
9. What do the ideas of Pestalozzi, Mursell, Bruner, Gagné, Gardner, and Gordon have in common?
10. What is unique about Gordon's learning sequence?
11. How does the Gordon learning skills sequence aid teaching more efficiently?
12. How does language learning parallel Gordon's learning sequence?
13. What is the role of Verbal Association in music learning?
14. What is the role of rote training in music learning?
15. When is it appropriate to introduce music notation?
16. What is the role of "playing by ear" in learning to play an instrument?

References

BLOOM, BENJAMIN S., ed. (1985). *Developing talent in young people*. New York: Ballantine Books.

———, and LAUREN A. SOSNIAK. (1981). Talent development vs. schooling. *Educational Leadership* 39(2), 86–90.

BRUNER, JEROME S. (1960). *The process of education.* Cambridge, MA: Harvard University Press.
———. (1966). *Toward a theory of instruction.* Cambridge, MA: Harvard University Press.
CAMPBELL, PATRICIA SHEHAN, and CAROL SCOTT-KASSNER. (1995). *Music in childhood.* New York: Schirmer Books.
GAGNÉ, ROBERT M. ([1965] 1977). *The conditions of learning.* New York: Holt, Rinehart and Winston, Inc.
GARDNER, HOWARD. (1983). *Frames of mind: The theory of multiple intelligences.* New York: Basic Books, Inc.
———. (1985). *The mind's new science.* New York: Basic Books, Inc.
———. (1991). *The unschooled mind.* New York: Basic Books, Inc.
———. (1993). *Multiple intelligences: The theory in practice.* New York: Basic Books, Inc.
GORDON, EDWIN E. (1971). *The psychology of music teaching.* Englewood Cliffs, NJ: Prentice-Hall, Inc.
———. (1993). *Learning sequences in music.* Chicago: GIA Publications, Inc.
HOLZ, EMIL A., and ROGER E. JACOBI. (1966). *Teaching band instruments to beginners.* Englewood Cliffs, NJ: Prentice-Hall, Inc.
MCPHERSON, GARY E. (1993). Factors and abilities influencing the development of visual, aural and creative performance skills in music and their educational implications. Ph.D. diss., University of Sydney, Australia, DAI 54/04-A, 1277. University Microfilms No. 9317278.
MEYER, LEONARD B. (1989). *Style and music: Theory, history, and ideology.* Philadelphia: University of Philadelphia Press.
MONROE, WILL S. (1907). *History of the Pestalozzian movement in the United States.* Syracuse: C. W. Bardeen; quoted in Charles Leonhard and Robert House. (1959). *Foundations and principles of music education.* New York: McGraw-Hill, Inc., 52–53.
MURSELL, JAMES L. (1958). Growth processes in music education. In *Basic concepts in music education: The fifty-seventh yearbook of the National Society for the Study of Education (Part I),* Nelson B. Henry, ed. Chicago: University of Chicago Press.
———, and MABELLE GLENN. (1931). *The psychology of school music teaching.* New York: Silver Burdett Co.
SIDNELL, ROBERT. (1973). *Building instructional programs in music education.* Englewood Cliffs, NJ: Prentice-Hall, Inc.
THORPE, LOUIS P. (1958). Learning theory and music teaching. In *Basic concepts in music education: The fifty-seventh yearbook of the National Society for the Study of Education (Part I),* Nelson B. Henry, ed. Chicago: University of Chicago Press.
VELLEMAN, BARRY L. (1978). Speaking of jazz. *Music Educators Journal* 65 (2), 28–31.

For Further Reading

RADOCY, RUDOLF E., and DAVID J. BOYLE. (1988). *Psychological foundations of musical behavior,* 2nd ed. Springfield, IL: Charles C. Thomas.
WILSON, FRANK R. (1986). *Tone deaf and all thumbs.* New York: Viking Penguin, Inc.

Teaching a Sense of Tonality

Awareness and control of pitch and intonation . . . [do] not seem to be an independent perceptual skill. Direct drill on pitch aware-ness is not likely to be found very fruitful in correcting bad intona-tion. This is because we actually hear and respond to pitch always in a tonal setting rather than in isolation. The way to get groups of performers or individuals to play or sing more perfectly on the pitch is to build up their feeling of tonality—for the functional relation-ship of each separate pitch to all the rest. (Mursell, 1943, p. 166)

A sixth-grade student spent the week practicing an assigned piece for trumpet. It was notated in G major in the book, but the student ignored the key signature and practiced all F-sharps as F-naturals throughout the week. The teacher noticed at the succeeding lesson that the student was unaware that the piece did not sound in the major mode. What is a probable reason for this problem?

Most traditional instruction of beginning instrumentalists excludes a developmental sequence for establishing a sense of tonality. (This is also true of many elementary general music programs.) What are the prerequisite steps for teaching the content of tonal music? How do teachers determine what should be taught next? Traditionally, empha-sis is placed on technical skill with the instruments, rhythm-reading skills, and association of fingerings with notation. Instrumentalists are often preoccupied with reading pitch notation as fingering cues at beginning stages of learning. Reading from note to note with appropri-ate fingerings does not efficiently develop a sense of tonality.

Instrumental students are allowed and encouraged to use instruments as tonal crutches by primarily associating notation with correct finger-ings—not the correct sound. As a result, there are scores of instru-mental performers who "can't perform without their music" and in fact can't perform *with* their music. Students need directed training to develop a sense of tonality that will in turn greatly aid their instru-mental performance. Instrumentalists should first audiate tonally and then compare the sounds produced on their instrument with that internalized model.

Defining a Sense of Tonality

Tonality is an important syntactical device in nearly all Western music. It is a "glue" that provides continuity and expectation in the music of our culture. Both Paul R. Farnsworth (1969) and Robert W. Lundin (1985) discuss the cultural basis of tonality in music and its subjective development in Western music over many centuries. More recent studies about enculturation and a sense of tonality are discussed fur-ther in books by Shuter-Dyson and Gabriel (1981) and by Radocy and Boyle (1988).

A sense of tonality is a learned phenomenon and requires tonal memory. Taylor (1976) examined the tonality strength (degree of per-ception of tonal center) in short melodies by utilizing information the-ory and concluded that perception of tonality is learned. In music, this framework of tonality helps one remember what has been heard and then allows anticipation on the basis of that which has become famil-iar. What is "known" is initially developed informally through listening to various types of music, often from radio, television, and tape or disc recordings. Understanding and expectation are enhanced by percep-tion of tonality in music. Meyer (1956, 1967) has written extensively on expectation in music, and how it aids understanding and organization.

A sense of tonality is, in effect, a sense of mode. Modes are based on various scale structures, which are arrangements of whole and half-steps. Although other connotations may be found, for our purposes tonality is synonymous with mode. Aural recognition of major, minor, dorian, mixolydian or other tonalities results from ease of perception of the tonal center of melodies and from chordal accompaniment. The resting tone (also called *home tone*, *key tone*, *tonic note*) is the tonal center for a given mode and is frequently the last tone of a melody. The two most common modes in Western music are major and minor. Songs occur with much less frequency in dorian, phrygian, lydian, and mixolydian modes. Of course, not all music in our culture has obvious resting tones to suggest specific tonalities. Composers of atonal and aleatoric music intentionally avoid feeling for tonal centers. The music used for beginning levels of singing and playing instruments is decidedly tonal in nature. It is generally agreed in practice that tonal music is taught and learned before other types are attempted.

Tonality should not be confused with *keyality*—the key letter name. Keyality is labeling a pitch perceived as the resting tone, regardless of mode. Key signatures must vary accordingly. "The key of A" is not a meaningful statement unless the mode is also named—A lydian, A dorian, A major, and so on. Key signatures by themselves do not indicate either the mode or the key name of a particular selection until the resting tone is identified. Authors of beginning instrumental method books often ignore or misunderstand this important consideration. Instrumental music selections are sometimes notated with incorrect key signatures. A typical example is a piece in D dorian (no flats or sharps) given the key signature of D minor (one flat) with all B-flats given natural signs throughout the piece. Another commonly found example is a tune in major mode with the resting tone of G notated with no key signature because no Fs occur in the melody. A key signature of four sharps is appropriate for E major, F-sharp dorian, G-sharp phrygian, A lydian, B mixolydian, and C-sharp minor (see Figure 3.1 for the various possibilities).

Any tonality or mode may have as its resting tone any of the twelve chromatic scale pitches. Key modulations within a melody occur when the tonal center shifts to a different pitch level. When an entire melody is assigned to a new pitch level (new resting-tone pitch) but the mode remains the same, it is commonly called transposition. Playing tunes at different pitch levels is greatly facilitated by a strong sense of tonality.

For instrumental students and teachers, some examples of demonstrating a sense of tonality include

- knowing when a played or sung pitch sounds right or wrong, i.e., whether or not the pitch "fits" with the pitches around it

- aurally recognizing the difference among songs in major or in minor mode
- anticipating the resting tone of a tune
- aurally recognizing the cadential sections of a piece
- experiencing tonal audiation, i.e., "hearing in your head" what the next pitches should be before they are sounded
- knowing the difference between playing through a piece to "see what it sounds like" and knowing how it should sound before playing it
- functioning tonally with musically trained ears, eyes, and fingers

Conversely, a sense of tonality is *not*

- matching instrument fingerings with written notes
- knowing the names of lines and spaces on the staff
- reading, spelling, and playing scales
- memorizing that major scales have half-steps between the third and fourth and the seventh and eighth scale degrees
- knowing how to spell chords
- recognizing the key name of a selection by its key signature

Research specific to instrumental music teaching and a sense of tonality is relatively sparse. Selected references are included throughout the remainder of this chapter with the intention of synthesizing research implications for instrumental music teaching.

Tonal Readiness

Beginning instrumentalists should be expected to have some aural concept of tonality. These tonal concepts result from exposure throughout childhood to recorded and live music performances, with perhaps some contribution from classroom general music. Most of the music that children have heard is in major tonality, and thus their aural concepts of other modes are more limited.

Extensive singing is probably the most important activity for developing of a sense of tonality and instrument readiness. In earliest childhood, children should be expected and encouraged to sing. Simple

Mode	Tonic Syllable															
Major	Do	C♭	G♭	D♭	A♭	E♭	B♭	F	C	G	D	A	E	B	F♯	C♯
Dorian	Re	D♭	A♭	E♭	B♭	F	C	G	D	A	E	B	F♯	C♯	G♯	D♯
Phrygian	Mi	E♭	B♭	F	C	G	D	A	E	B	F♯	C♯	G♯	D♯	A♯	E♯
Lydian	Fa	F♭	C♭	G♭	D♭	A♭	E♭	B♭	F	C	G	D	A	E	B	F♯
Mixolydian	Sol	G♭	D♭	A♭	E♭	B♭	F	C	G	D	A	E	B	F♯	C♯	G♯
Minor	La	A♭	E♭	B♭	F	C	G	D	A	E	B	F♯	C♯	G♯	D♯	A♯

Figure 3.1   KEY AND MODE NAMES FOR KEY SIGNATURES

tunes and melodies with words should be learned by rote. Singing along with recordings of children's songs (preferably sung in tune by children) is a helpful activity. Parents should sing regularly to and with their children.

Beginning instrumentalists may or may not have a repertoire of familiar songs that they can sing, so they may need to learn additional songs through singing prior to instrumental experience and continue to learn new songs while studying an instrument. Lessons and rehearsals should include frequent singing activities.

It is important to recognize that unless physically disabled, anyone can sing. Singing is an acquired skill. Many instrumental students may have singing-voice problems which have gone uncorrected. Instrumental teachers must also be voice teachers and know how to work with children's voice problems. It is beyond the scope of this book to elaborate on techniques for dealing with singing-voice training and correcting, but the reader is especially urged to consult the book *Teaching Kids to Sing* by Kenneth Phillips (1992) for assistance.

Evidence suggests that without a developed sense of tonality it is difficult to sing in tune. Further, most instrumentalists play consistently in tune if they sing in tune. Harris's (1977) evidence supports this assumption; he found that vocalization improved instrumental intonation of junior and senior high school instrumentalists. An instrument may be used as a means to express tonality, but a performer must audiate what is to be played and later what is seen in notation in order to play in tune. McGarry (1967), Elliott (1972), and Schlacks (1981) each reported significant effects of vocalization with various groups of instrumental achievers; Dunlap (1989), however, found no differences between elementary beginners taught with tonal patterns and singing and those taught with tonal patterns and no singing.

Children should also have opportunities for repeated listening to recorded songs with melodies in various modes and with appealing lyrics. It is especially helpful to have recorded examples of materials to be performed. Suzuki (1969) gives much importance to aural training of stringed-instrument players through use of recorded models of tonal music. His purposes are twofold: to develop familiarity with music to be played and to establish a model of tone quality. A third result is aural reinforcement of tonal understandings. Sperti (1970) included recorded materials in an adaptation of Suzuki's techniques for teaching beginning clarinetists. Achievement of clarinet students with access to recorded materials was superior to those without recorded models.

Listening and singing constitute the A/O foundation on which a sense of tonality and audiation is established. Songs that students already know through singing are the most effective musical material for beginning instrumentalists. This allows an instrument to become an extension of the voice. An instrument becomes a means for musical self-expression rather than only a device to manipulate.

Tunes to be performed on instruments should include lyrics, which facilitate singing and expressiveness. Words also help draw attention to appropriate phrasing and act as reference points for explanations and directions. Unfortunately, most training materials for instrumentalists do not include lyrics.

Beginning instrumental instruction should regularly include singing tunes before they are played. Students should then be encouraged to play familiar simple tunes "by ear" at many different pitch levels. Playing tunes without reference to notation is a critical activity to help focusing on expressive sounds. Fingerings and range expansion can be accomplished without additional material; a musical reason will exist for learning new fingerings. Sound should be emphasized before symbols—students should regularly perform by ear without notation, especially during beginning stages. Two techniques for developing tonal audiation skills are: 1) students are asked to begin singing a familiar song and at the teacher's cue, stop singing aloud but continue "thinking the melody" in tempo until the teacher cues their singing aloud again; and 2) students are asked to perform a familiar tune by ear with their instruments and at the teacher's cue, stop sounding the melody but continue doing the fingerings while "thinking the melody" in tempo until the teacher cues their reentry with their instrument sounds.

Instrumental music programs should have direct connections with elementary general music content—not an original idea but certainly one not evident in most school music programs. Singing in general-music classes can be an important basis for instrumental programs. All children should first develop their singing voices for expressing themselves musically. Many of these songs may be performed without notation on instruments, and they may be arranged and adapted to provide a familiar repertoire of aural/oral models for instrumental performance.

Recall the experience of using your instrument to sight-read a selection which you had heard before but had not seen previously in notation. Usually, the sight-reading goes quite well because the sounds produced on the instrument can be compared with the internalized, audiated model. On the other hand, when asked to sight-read completely unfamiliar music, the difficulty of the task increases dramatically depending on how much musical meaning the performer gives *to* the notation. Beginning instrumentalists should not be asked to read totally unfamiliar music without first developing their musical readiness to read notation meaningfully. Otherwise, students become button-pushers to whom notation indicates only what fingers to put down rather than what sounds are desired.

Initial Tonal Content

It is generally believed that a sense of tonality is initially developed through an aural affinity for a tonal center or final resting tone. This tone is also known as the key-tone or tonic and is defined as the first scale-tone of a given mode. Underlying harmonic structures also provide important aural cues to tonality recognition.

Drawing attention to the final resting tone of many songs sung or played is an important initial activity. Students should be trained to recognize aurally where the resting tone occurs in tunes of various modes. Techniques might include: 1) requesting students to sing and/or play the resting tone to an incomplete phrase or tune; 2) listening to recordings or to the performance of other students or the teacher and recognizing what pitch is the resting tone and indicating when it occurs; 3) having one or two students play only when the resting tone occurs while others sing the tune; and 4) counting how many times the resting tone occurs at phrase endings while hearing or playing a song.

Tonic arpeggios that are sung and/or played prior to or following the performances of songs are helpful for establishing a sense of mode. In the following examples and in Table 3.1, the capital letters indicate movable *do* syllables. The lines above or below the syllable letters indicate the pitch direction from the previous syllable. Singing or playing D M̄ S̄ M̲ D̲ or extending to D M̄ S̄ M̲ D̲ T̲ D̄ or D R̄ M F̄ S̄ L̄ S̲ M̲ D̲ T̲ D̄ provides a "home base" for major-mode songs. Use L D̄M̄D̲ L or L D̄M̄D̲ L̲ S̲i L̄ or L T̄ D̄R̄ M̄F̄ M̲ D̲ L̲ S̲i L̄ with harmonic minor. For those unfamiliar with correct syllable pronunciation, they are phonetically pronounced: *do* = doe, *re* = ray, *mi* = mee, *fa* = fah, *so* = so, *la* = lah, *ti* = tee.

Table 3.1 includes tonic arpeggios for six different modes. In each case, the longest arpeggio includes all the characteristic sounds of the particular mode. Students should first be taught to sing the arpeggios by rote and then to play them without notation at as many pitch levels as their range allows. A useful lesson activity is to ask students on hearing, singing, or playing a major or minor song, "Is it a D M̄ S̄ or a L D̄ M̄ [sing the syllables] song?" and, "Which sounds correct?"

TABLE 3.1

TONIC ARPEGGIOS FOR SIX MODES

Mode	Arpeggio
Major	D M̄ S̄ M D
	D M̄ S̄ M D T D̄
	D R̄ M F S̄ L̄ S M D T D̄
Dorian	R F̄ L̄ R
	R F̄ L̄ R D R̄
	R M̄ F S̄ L̄ T L F R D R̄
Phrygian	M S̄ T S M
	M S̄ T S M R M̄
	M F̄ S̄ L T D̄ T S M R M̄
Lydian	F L̄ D̄L F
	F L̄ D̄L F M F̄
	F S̄ L̄ T D̄ R D̄ L F M F̄
Mixolydian	S T̄ R̄ T S
	S T̄ R̄ T S F S̄
	S L̄ T D̄ R M̄ R T S F S̄
Minor	L D̄ M̄ D L
	L D̄ M̄ D L Si L̄
	L T̄ D̄ R M̄ F M D L Si L̄

Both major- and minor-mode songs should be used regularly in instrumental instruction so comparisons may be made between the sounds of the two modes. After a considerable repertoire of major and minor songs can be performed, introduce songs in dorian and mixolydian. Later on, include songs in phrygian and lydian modes. Songs in modes other than major and minor may be located in folk music from many European countries and in American Indian music for use as supplementary material. Music from other countries of the world is also appropriate for expanding tonality concepts beyond major and minor modes. Unfortunately, most instrumental materials include far too many major-mode songs in proportion to those in minor, and few songs in other modes are included.

Using Movable *Do*

Various forms of movable *do* techniques have been found in music teaching in this country since the time of Lowell Mason in the mid-1800s. When used, it has been more widespread in classroom general music than instrumental music teaching. Dykema and Cundiff (1955) typify much of the practice of movable *do* use in this country through the mid-1900s in their observation that

> Properly used, scale syllable names: (1) Furnish a correct and help-ful method of establishing early in the learner's consciousness, com-mand of the intervals, both step-wise and in leaps, of the major scale, and eventually of all scales. (2) Make music reading in any key equally feasible, because the relative tone relations of scale tones and their names are uniform in all keys. When the correct location of the key or central tone (*do*) is established from the key signature, all other tones naturally fall into the familiar pattern used in every key. (3) Introduce chromatic tones with simple spe-cial names which are logically related to the names and musical qualities of the major scale tones. (4) Clarify concepts of transposi-tion and modulation by introducing the transitional tones gradually in easily performed musical material. (5) Form the simplest method now available for enabling the grade teacher to teach and supervise music reading, as has been widely demonstrated by its successful use in schools where there was no other musical equipment than pitch-pipe and music books. (6) Correlate with writing down music heard or originated, and with playing by ear. Many instrumental teachers use them as a means of helping their pupil transpose sim-ple compositions into a variety of keys. (p. 70)

Of the various popular techniques including note names, fixed *do*, and numbers, the movable *do* system is the most efficient means of attaching tonal meaning to patterns of pitches for the purpose of developing a tonal pattern vocabulary and a sense of tonality. The vowel sounds of the syllables are easily sung, and singing only one syllable per tone eliminates any possible rhythmic complication. In the movable *do* system, syllables are assigned to modes as follows with the first syllable being the resting tone:

Major	DO *re mi fa so la ti do*
Dorian	RE *mi fa so la ti do re*
Phrygian	MI *fa so la ti do re mi*
Lydian	FA *so la ti do re mi fa*
Mixolydian	SO *la ti do re mi fa so*
Minor	LA *ti do re mi fa si la*

Notice that in minor mode *si* is used to provide the harmonic form commonly used in song literature. An important advantage of the movable *do* system is that by using a different syllable for the resting tone of each mode, the resulting sequence of whole and half steps is automatically correct for each mode without chromatic alteration of syllables.

Another advantage of movable *do* syllables is the availability of a systematic and unique monosyllabic set of syllables for chromatic and accidental pitches. Raising pitches by half-steps is accomplished by

do(di) re(ri) mi fa(fi) so(si) ti do

Lowering pitches by half-steps occurs as follows:

do ti(te) la(le) so(se) fa mi(me) re(ra) do

Chromatic syllables are not used for raised *mi* and *ti* or for lowered *fa* and *do* because of the half-step interval between *mi* and *fa* and between *ti* and *do*. They are also unnecessary because beginning song literature rarely includes those chromatic alterations.

Changes to relative and parallel modes are easily accomplished without chromatic syllables. To move to a relative mode, keep the key signature constant and start on the pitch with the syllable for the resting tone of the relative mode. (Given a key signature of three flats, E-flat is *do* and is the resting tone in the E-flat major mode. To move to the relative minor mode, C minor, keep the key signature of three flats and begin the scale on C, which is *la*.) To move to a parallel mode, keep the pitch the same for the resting tone in both modes and change the key signature and resting-tone syllable appropriate to the new parallel mode. (Given a key signature of three flats for E-flat major, E-flat is *do* and is the resting tone. To move to the parallel minor mode, E-flat minor, E-flat is now renamed *la*, the resting tone, and the key signature must become six flats where *do* is G-flat.) Review Figure 3.1 for relationships among keys, syllables, and mode resting tones. Intervallic distances between syllables remain constant regardless of mode.

As suggested in Dykema and Cundiff's point 6 above, tonal syllables expedite playing by ear, taking dictation, and composing/arranging. The association of the syllables with the sounds of tonal patterns facilitates audiation and works as an encoding process for sounds that may then be represented with notation. This is a gradual learning process that needs to be reinforced and expanded throughout instrumental training.

Initial use of tonal syllables should be with the *sound* and *not notation* of two to five tone patterns. The tonal syllables become, in effect, the "words" for sound-pattern relationships that appear again and again in melodies at various pitch levels. The tonal patterns become the building blocks for a sense of tonality and facility with pitch relationships.

Another reason to use movable *do* is to facilitate audiation and theoretical understanding of scales in all modes. The syllable sequence includes two built-in half-steps, *mi-fa* and *ti-do*, and the intervals between other adjacent syllables are whole-steps. The correct order of half- and whole-steps for the scale of any mode occurs automatically by simply choosing the appropriate resting-tone syllable for the mode. Refer again to Figure 3.1 for the relationships among modes, key signatures, and resting-tone syllables. This information is obviously not an initial learning activity but becomes appropriate after discrimination learning occurs.

Students should *not* be expected to sing through entire melodies using tonal syllables in melodic rhythm. Initially, tonal syllables should be reserved for learning new patterns and for reinforcing previously learned patterns. Advanced students with a developed vocabulary of tonal patterns may wish to sing syllables melodically throughout entire familiar tunes, but this is not an initial learning activity nor an end in itself.

Echo-singing and echo-playing are essential techniques for building a vocabulary of tonal patterns with syllables and without notation. The verbal association process is accomplished with the movable *do* syllables. Syllables should be first echo-sung for the patterns without notation. Patterns may then be performed instrumentally at different pitch levels. Introducing the tonic major arpeggio pattern (D M̄ S̄) without notation would proceed as follows:

TEACHER	STUDENT
1. Sings D M̄ S̄ with lu, lu, lu	echo-sings lu, lu, lu
2. Sings/plays pitches	echo-plays
3. Sings D M̄ S̄	echo-sings D M̄ S̄
4. Sings D M̄ S̄ with lu, lu, lu	sings D M̄ S̄
5. Sings D M̄ S̄	plays D M̄ S̄
6. Gives new fingerings if necessary, asks for D M̄ S̄ with new pitches	plays D M̄ S̄ with new pitches

Again, it is important to recognize the purpose for using tonal syllables—to verbally associate with sounds of melodic patterns of two to five tones and to develop a vocabulary of tonal-pattern sounds that may be recognized and retrieved through their functional syllable labels. Often as a result of college music-theory training, music teachers attempt to use numbers as an association with pitches. What is ignored is that most music theorists do not intend to develop a vocabulary of patterns and sense of tonality through the use of numbers. Instead, they are visually associating numbers with scale degrees concurrent with music notation that is already familiar to their students. Little or no consideration is given to the difficulties in singing numbers or the preestablished connotations and associations of numbers with counting and mathematics.

Building a Tonal-Pattern Vocabulary

A vocabulary of tonal patterns should be taught with aural resting-tone recognition and association of tunes with major and minor tonic arpeggios. Tonal patterns are groups of two to five pitches exclusive of repeated tones that are related to and derived from underlying harmonic function. Tonal patterns should be sung or played in a steady, moderate tempo without other rhythmic interaction to assure focus on pitch rather than rhythms. The determination of tonal-pattern parameters within a melody is somewhat arbitrary. Common sense with attention to pitch direction, phrasing, and harmonic function provides workable criteria. The following song text excerpt has the tonal patterns indicated by tonal syllables underneath the words. Pattern length is indicated by slashes (/).

Hot	cross	buns, / hot	cross	buns, /
M	R	D / M	R	D /

One	a-pen-ny,	two a-pen-ny, /	hot	cross	buns,	/
D		R̄ /	M	R	D	/

Notice that in this particular song, two- or three-tone patterns are arbitrarily chosen to fit with the phrase structure. Melodic repetitions of same pitches are intentionally ignored within each pattern. "Hot Cross Buns" is a particularly useful song because of its limited range and pattern content. It is not necessary to teach every tonal pattern in more complex melodies before or after singing and playing the tune.

MacKnight (1975) investigated the effect of tonal pattern training on achievement of beginning instrumentalists. She concluded that tonal pattern training produces a higher average level of music achievement than does note identification training. Grutzmacher (1987) used tonal patterns and movable *do* with a group of beginning instrumentalists (grades 5–6) for fourteen weeks and taught a comparable group without pattern training. She found that the group trained with patterns was more proficient with aural recognition of major and minor and with melodic sight-reading. Extensive research on development of a tonal pattern taxonomy was done by Gordon (1993). His research provides information concerning the perceptual difficulty and implied harmonic function of tonal patterns. Music teaching and learning may be greatly enhanced when tonal pattern training is based on an effective sequence of pattern content.

Patterns are first introduced to students through echo-singing with a neutral, singable syllable such as "loo." The first patterns of two to five tones to be taught should be taken from the tonic chord (e.g., D M̄ S̄, D M̄ D in major). Diatonic patterns outlined by chord tones may also be used (e.g., D R̄ M̄, D M̄F S̄ in major). Students may also echo-play patterns when given correct fingerings.

Tonal-Pattern Content

Examples of tonal patterns are displayed in Figure 3.2. The patterns shown are for major and minor modes. The basic patterns consist of pitches from the tonic, dominant seventh, and subdominant chords. Patterns from the dominant seventh and subdominant chords should be taught after a number of tonic chord patterns are learned. When working with other than tonic chord patterns, be certain to establish the tonality by first echoing tonic arpeggios.

It is often helpful (especially for woodwinds, strings, and keyboards) to use tonal patterns that include appropriate passing tones within the given key. Moving diatonically is an aid in developing smooth fingering technique. Playing in tune and awareness of harmonic function is enhanced when diatonic patterns begin and end with chord tones. Typical beginning patterns in major include D R̄ M, M R̲ D̲, D R̄ M F S̄, S F̲ M̲ R̲ D̲, S L̲ T̄ D̲, and in minor, L T̄ D̲, D T̲ L, L T̄ D R̄ M, M R̲ D̲ T̲ L, M F̄ S̄ L.

Tonal patterns based on supertonic, submediant, and mediant chords may be introduced after basic patterns are learned. Patterns with accidentals and chromatics may also be included as students become more proficient.

More Tonal Pattern Teaching Techniques

As soon as students can play a few patterns, they should be encouraged to make up their own tunes using the patterns. This may be accomplished through singing or playing a chained-together series of familiar patterns with simple articulations and rhythms. Students should be discouraged from playing randomly chosen series of fingerings without first audiating the sounds. Improvisation skills begin with having something to say through the instrument. Note that these activities need not be delayed until later stages of proficiency.

Pitch letter names should be associated initially with fingerings and used as verbal reference points to fingering locations when playing tonal patterns. This allows instructions such as "Play D M̄ S̄ with *do* as G; with *do* as F, and *do* as A." Beginning instrumentalists should not be required to learn the names of staff lines and spaces until they have worked aurally with tonal syllables and patterns. Names of written notes are learned functionally as familiar tonal patterns are associated with symbols. Letter names are also used to label instrument fingerings.

56

CHAPTER 3

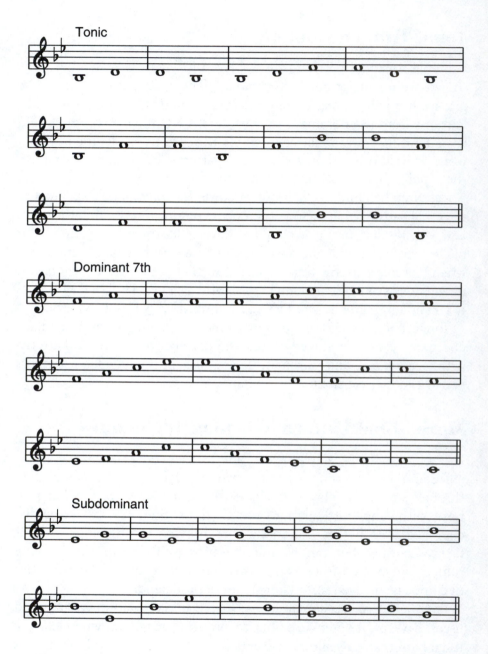

Figure 3.2a   SELECTED BEGINNING TONAL PATTERNS
FOR MAJOR MODE

Figure 3.2b   SELECTED BEGINNING TONAL
PATTERNS FOR MINOR MODE

Saxophone class singing and fingering

Tonal syllables must not be exclusively associated with fingerings or letter names whenever new patterns are introduced. It is important to learn any given tonal pattern at more than one pitch level concurrently so that fingerings are not always associated with particular tonal syllables. Practice assignments should include patterns at two or more pitch levels. Transposition becomes an easy process when a tonal-pattern vocabulary is practiced at many pitch levels. Beginning songs should also be regularly performed at more than one starting pitch, and new fingerings should be given as needed. With the exception of keyboard instruments, the initial constraint is range and not what keys or fingerings are introduced.

In instrumental training, tonal patterns should generally relate directly to tunes that are sung and played. After learning to sing and play a tune, tonal patterns may be extracted and practiced alone. It is not necessary to deal with all possible patterns in a melody. Students might be asked to discover the frequency of a given pattern within a song or to recall other familiar songs that incorporate the same pattern (PS). Other activities might include 1) organizing patterns in the order in which they occur in a particular song (PS or CS); 2) rearranging the

Student providing tonal patterns for class echoing

tonal patterns of a familiar song to create a different song (C/I); and 3) altering patterns within a song to create melodic variation (C/I). This should first be done aurally with syllables and later with notation.

Consider the following tonal patterns: D S̄ L̄ S, F M R D, S F M R. Students could echo-sing and -play the patterns and then be asked if they know any songs that include these patterns. "Twinkle, Twinkle, Little Star" could then be sung and/or played. The three patterns may be recognized as constituting the melody of the song.

Tonal patterns may also be used as ostinatos for simple tunes. Students may be encouraged to discover which patterns function as ostinatos with specific tunes. Small sections of rounds may be used as tonal ostinatos to accompany the melody of the round.

The development of a sense of tonality and a tonal-pattern vocabulary is enhanced by the use of harmonic accompaniments. Consider using the guitar, autoharp, or keyboard on a regular basis for providing harmonic accompaniments to instrumental lesson material. A cadential chord progression used as an introduction to melodies can establish the mode or tonality and the starting pitch for the performers. The tonal function of any given pitch in a melody is immediately more obvious if harmonic reinforcement is available. Playing in tune becomes generally easier and more accurate with chordal accompaniment.

Considering the first three levels of Gordon's learning skills sequence and teaching tonal patterns, examples of Aural/Oral and Verbal Association activities are included above. Some additional specific suggestions for Partial Synthesis activities to be used before notation for patterns is introduced include the following:

1. Raise a hand when aurally recognizing a familiar pattern in a familiar song
2. Aurally count how many times a given pattern occurs in a familiar song
3. Recognize familiar patterns in familiar songs while singing or playing them
4. Recognize and name the tonality of a familiar song that contains a given pattern while listening, singing, or playing the song
5. Chain familiar tonal patterns together through singing or playing to reconstruct a familiar song
6. Name, sing, or play songs that contain a given pattern.

Arpeggio Worksheet

An arpeggio worksheet is shown in Figure 3.3. Columns of syllables should be read as arpeggios from bottom to top to bottom—D M̄ S̄ M̲ D, D F̄ L̲ F̲ D, etc. Different students in a class may then simultaneously sing or play the horizontal lines—S L̄ S S S, M F̄ M̲ F̄ M, D D D T̲ D to sound the chord progression. Each chord of simultaneously sounded columns of syllables may be repeated before moving to the next one. Holding up one, four, or five fingers as a visual cue for a chord permits changing the order of chords during performance. The number of repetitions of each chord may be predetermined or indicated during performance. Simple tunes may be chordally accompanied by a minimum of three class members while the teacher or another student indicates appropriate chord changes. Students should determine aurally if the chord changes sound appropriate and make changes as desired. Individuals may improvise melodic patterns on underlying chord progressions provided by the class. The arpeggios and chord accompaniments in both major and minor should be emphasized and eventually learned in all keys.

```
        L                               I CAN PLAY THIS
  S             S     S     S            WITH DO AS
                                          _____
        F             F                   _____
  M             M           M             _____
                                          _____
                                          _____
               (R)                        _____
  D       D     D           D             _____
                T                         _____

  I      IV     I    V7     I
_____

        F
  M             M     M     M            I CAN PLAY THIS
                                         WITH LA AS
                                          _____
        R             R                   _____
  D             D           D             _____
                                          _____
                                          _____
               (T)                        _____
  L       L     L           L             _____
               Si                         _____

  i      iv     i    V7     i
```

Figure 3.3   ARPEGGIO WORKSHEET

Dialogue Techniques

A dialogue is basically a statement and response. A dialogue response answers the statement with a different or altered response whereas an echo-technique response is an exact repetition of the statement. Dialogue techniques are especially useful for developing tonal pattern vocabularies. Variations include: 1) the student performs the A section of a simple tonal pattern rondo while the teacher intersperses contrasting patterns; 2) the teacher performs the A section of a simple tonal pattern rondo while individual students intersperse contrasting patterns; and 3) students each perform a chain of different patterns without teacher interaction. The patterns may be sung with syllables or played with instruments. Individual differences may be met within class groupings.

Many variations are possible, and many levels of difficulty may be established by altering the content and task. Content may be drilled with dialogue techniques, since students enjoy the process. The learning sequence level may be varied while the rhythm or tonal pattern content remains the same, or pattern content may be varied while learning sequence level remains the same. Individual differences are easily managed because students can respond within their own vocabulary knowledge.

Dialogue techniques are especially effective as measurement techniques in which many students can individually demonstrate skill and knowledge in brief periods of time. Diagnosis of student achievement levels and skills is facilitated. For example, during a dialogue activity, the teacher discovers that a particular student can provide the correct tonal syllables (VA) for a given pattern but is unable to read the pattern. The student may know the names of the written symbols but cannot read and sing them with accurate pitches. This indicates a need for more practice with the syllables (VA) before further reading of the pattern.

The examples listed below are for tonal dialogues. The statements (S) may be provided by the teacher or by a student leader. Tonal pattern dialogues should avoid rhythmic interaction and normally consist of two to five pitches in each statement and response. Patterns should relate to tonic function major and minor initially and then to dominant and subdominant chords before becoming more complex, either by relating to lesser-used chords or to more than one chord in a pattern. Examples of tonal pattern dialogue formats are:

1. (S) Sing pattern on neutral syllable ("loo") (Aural/Oral recall or creativity)

    (R) Sing a different pattern with neutral syllable (A/O recall or creativity)

2. (S) Sing pattern on neutral syllable ("loo") (A/O recall or creativity)

    (R) Sing same pattern with syllables (VA)

3. (S) Sing pattern with syllables (VA or if read, SA)
    (R) Sing different patterns with syllables (VA creativity)
4. (S) Sing pattern on neutral syllable (A/O recall or creativity)
    (R) Play a different pattern (A/O recall or creativity)
5. (S) Play pattern (A/O recall or creativity)
    (R) Sing same pattern with syllables (VA), then play it (A/O)
6. (S) Play pattern (A/O recall or creativity)
    (R) Play a different pattern (A/O recall or creativity)

Reading Tonal Notation

> Knowledge of musical practice, gained primarily through study of
> an instrument using conventional notation, produces a surprisingly
> limited understanding of musical representation. . . . The lessons
> learned by studying an instrument appear not to transfer to nota-
> tion, particularly with regard to pitch. The study of an instrument
> often involves using the notation system to indicate when and
> where to put fingers on the string, the keyboard, and so forth. This
> does not build an internal representation system that can be used
> independently of the instrument. (Davidson, Scripp, and Welsh,
> 1988, pp. 68–69)

Most traditional approaches to instrumental training begin with the
association of fingerings and notation; the symbols being only fingering cues rather than sound cues also. Students are seldom, if at all,
expected to improvise or perform by ear. This visual process is often
nonmusical, boring, difficult, and musically unproductive for students.
Self-expression and audiation through instrument performance occurs
only minimally for large numbers of students. And music teachers
wonder why so few students are motivated to continue playing their
instruments into adulthood.

The readiness for reading music notation is demonstrated when simple tunes can be sung and played and when tonal patterns can be performed with syllables and instruments. Fingering patterns should first
be associated aurally with tonal patterns. Students should perform a
repertoire of simple songs by ear. These songs and tonal patterns that
have been performed without notation should be the first examples to

be seen with notation. The intention is to associate musical sounds with notation, not to attempt to extract musical sounds from notation.

The readiness sequence for reading tonal symbols begins with rote singing and playing of simple tunes and tonal patterns as described in earlier sections of this chapter. A critical interim step is the association of movable *do* syllables with the functional sound of tonal patterns. Students are ready to read the patterns when they can associate and sing the correct syllables with sounded patterns. A useful check is to sound a pattern without syllables and have students respond by singing the pattern with correct syllables. It is possible at this point to attach musical meaning to notation. The symbols are then representative of the tonal pattern vocabulary and are visual cues for specific fingerings, a process analogous to learning to speak before learning to read. The sequence for moving from syllable-association sounds to notation for a given familiar pattern could be as follows:

TEACHER	STUDENT
Sings M R̲ D̲	Echo-sings M R̲ D̲
Plays M R̲ D̲	Echo-plays M R̲ D̲
Sings lu (M), lu (R̲), lu (D̲)	Echo-sings M R̲ D̲
Shows notation for M R̲ D̲	Sings M R̲ D̲, plays M R̲ D̲
New notation for M R̲ D̲	Sings M R̲ D̲, plays M R̲ D̲

The pattern should be shown and learned in a new key as soon as students can consistently read it in the familiar key. Students should also copy notation of familiar patterns as a prerequisite to tonal dictation and composition.

It is not necessary to precede reading music notation with reading other less exact or different representations of pitches or melodic direction. This is analogous to insisting that children should learn to read a pre-alphabet set of symbols before learning the real alphabet symbols. When first reading music, special attention should be drawn to "on the line," meaning the line runs *through* the note head, and "in the space," meaning the note head is *between* lines, not on the line. These concepts are contradictory to what is taught in language reading and may otherwise confuse students. Reading music notation is appropriate after tonal readiness has been acquired.

One of the most effective and practical techniques for teaching music reading is the use of flash cards of familiar tonal patterns. Gradually introduce familiar patterns in various keys in major and minor on flash cards. Choice of keys should depend on appropriate instrument ranges. Each card should include a correct key signature, which assures the correct determination of *do*. Cards should be organized by chord function (tonic, dominant-seventh, subdominant, and so on for major and minor) of patterns within keys. Refer back to Figure 3.2 for examples of possible patterns to be placed on flash cards in various major and minor keys.

Pitch symbols should be called by letter names as they are associated with lines and spaces in pattern configurations on the flash cards. Fingerings that have been called by note names are then easily associated with staff notation, and the symbols representing audiated patterns are associated with the sound.

Activities with flash cards may include singing with correct syllables; singing correct syllables while doing correct fingerings on the instrument; playing patterns on the cards; recognizing patterns in notated songs that match the flash card patterns; creating new tunes by organizing various series of cards; recognizing which cards are being performed by other students; and copying notation from cards. These activities may take place in class or individual lessons or in large rehearsal groups. Brief but regular practice with flash cards of patterns that appear in familiar tunes is an important means toward developing tonal vocabulary and a sense of tonality.

Instrumentalists need to know how to interpret key signatures after music reading begins. Key signatures can give musical information if thought of as *do* signatures, i.e., symbols that visually locate the line or space for *do*. *Do* is located with sharp key signatures by beginning with the sharp sign farthest right as number one and counting down lines and spaces to seven. A helpful memory aid is to associate the sharp sign with a tic-tac-toe grid and say, "Tic-tac-toe, seven down to go." In flat key signatures, begin with the flat sign farthest right as number one and count down lines and spaces to four (or the next to the last flat in key signatures with more than one flat). Again, a memory aid is to associate a flat sign with the letter *b* and say, "When you see *b*'s, count down four please." Counting down to *do* rather than up visually places the note for *do* on the staff and in the correct range for beginners. After introducing key signatures with more than two flats, students may also be taught that *do* is located by the next to the last flat in the key signature. The location of C as *do* must be memorized for the key signature of no sharps or flats.

The location of the tone for any tonal syllable is easily interpreted after *do* is located. Students should become aware of some of the visual relationships of pitches on the staff by observing that when *do* is on a line, *mi* and *so* are on the next lines above; when *do* is in a space, *mi* and *so* are in the next spaces above; when *do* is on a line, the *do* an octave above is in a space; and when *do* is in a space, the *do* an octave above is on a line.

The letter name of the tonic resting tone becomes the key name, and the tonal syllable for the tonic resting tone indicates the mode name. For example, resting tone is Ab and *re* = Ab dorian (six flats); resting tone is B and *la* = B minor (two sharps); resting tone is B and *so* = B mixolydian (four sharps). See Figure 3.1 for comparisons. Note the advantage of using different movable *do* tonal syllables for the tonic of each mode when more than mode is taught and when key signatures are introduced. The order of sharps and flats in a key signature needs to be memorized. A mnemonic device useful for the order of sharps is "Fat Cats Get Drowsy After Eating Birds." The order of flats may be learned as the reverse of the sharps. Students often enjoy devising their own mnemonics for the sequence of sharps and flats in key signatures.

Reading unfamiliar music (sight-reading) is basically recognizing familiar patterns in new settings. Music for sight-reading is of an appropriate difficulty level when the majority of patterns are familiar. This allows success and motivation for most students. After students begin to read songs that they can already sing and play, opportunities for reading unfamiliar songs of the same difficulty level must be provided on a regular basis. Generalizing from the known to the unknown is facilitated through this practice. A helpful ongoing lesson assignment is for students to choose and prepare for performance a song of their choice from a song-collection book. The interaction of rhythm and tonal patterns with sight-reading is discussed further in Chapters 4 and 5.

It is essential that as students begin to read music, they also write music notation. Learning to read and write concurrently develops understanding of symbols for musical sounds more fully and encourages manipulation of the symbols through arranging and composition. The mechanics of writing music may be acquired by careful copying of tonal flash cards and simple familiar tunes. Tunes learned in one key should be written and performed in new keys. Students can compose new endings or variations of tunes, or compose settings for simple poems. Regular written assignments are appropriate when music reading begins. Dictation exercises of patterns and tunes are appropriate as students gain writing facility. Computer software programs for music notation are also helpful in motivating and facilitating student composing and arranging.

When beginning notation reading, movable *do* syllables are the verbal associations with familiar tonal patterns that are now represented by symbols. The syllables should not be used to sing through entire melodies but should be restricted for tonal pattern identification. The intent is for students to develop audiation facility (to hear what they see) without overtly thinking of each individual note or tonal syllable. Eventually, tonal syllables are internalized and students operate musically without consciously thinking about the syllables. New patterns or difficult patterns may continue to be introduced with syllable reference. This is analogous to what occurs in language reading when one no longer reads individual letters or words but instead reads phrases as expressions of meaning.

Because activities for Composite Synthesis are frequently ignored, here is a brief list of some possible student tasks to consider when working with pitch notation:

1. Visually recognize familiar patterns in familiar songs in notation and circle them
2. Visually count how many times a given pattern occurs in a familiar song
3. Recognize familiar patterns in familiar songs while singing or playing them from notation
4. Recognize the tonality of a familiar song which contains familiar patterns while listening, singing, or playing with notation
5. Chain familiar patterns together through singing or playing to reconstruct a familiar song with notation
6. Name, sing, or play songs that contain a given pattern with notation

Twinkle, Twinkle, Little Star

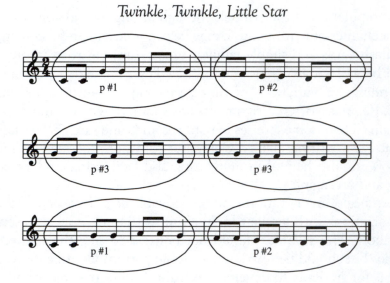

Figure 3.4   COMPOSITE SYNTHESIS EXAMPLE

Figure 3.4 contains an example of Composite Synthesis activities with a familiar song.

Assignment:

Wherever you see D S̄ L̄ S, circle it and mark as P#1. Wherever you see F M R D, circle it and mark as P#2.

Wherever you see S F M R, circle it and mark as P#3.

Perform the piece with your instrument.

Here, as a summary example, is a list of activities that follow the Gordon learning skills sequence in teaching a tonal pattern through the discrimination level of Composite Synthesis.

Given the *sound* of (specify a tonal pattern), students will

• echo-sing the pattern using "loo" (A/O)

• echo-sing with movable *do* syllables (VA)

• hear the pattern when sung on "loo" and respond by singing the correct tonal syllables (VA)

• echo-sing with movable *do* syllables while using a correct set of fingerings (VA)

- echo-perform the pattern with an instrument (VA)
- name a familiar song that contains the pattern (PS)

Given the *notation* of (specify a tonal pattern), students will

- sing the pattern using tonal syllables (SA)
- sing and demonstrate correct fingerings without playing (SA)
- perform the pattern with an instrument (SA)
- locate the pattern within the notation of a familiar song (CS)

Other Modes

It was mentioned earlier in this chapter that songs in modes other than major and minor should also be taught and learned as a part of instrumental music. Singing and playing songs in several different modes increases tonal vocabularies and aids a sense of tonality. When students are reading tunes in major and minor, it is appropriate to begin singing songs and learning patterns in other modes. Dorian, a minor-related mode, and mixolydian, a major-related mode, should be introduced next. After dorian and mixolydian songs are established, introduce material in phrygian and lydian. The sequence for introducing songs and tonal patterns in other modes is the same as for major and minor. Songs should be sung and played; tonic arpeggios with correct syllables should be learned (see Table 3.1); and tonal patterns relating to chords (see Figure 3.2) should be taught. Notation should be gradually introduced for familiar songs and patterns.

Switching Modes

Without reference to notation, an especially useful technique is to sing or play the same song in two or more modes. For example, students might first learn and perform "Are You Sleeping" in major and then switch it to minor. Be aware of characteristic pitches of the new mode in song melodies when determining what songs may be switched to what modes. For example, a natural minor melody without the sixth degree of the minor scale cannot be changed to dorian; a major melody without the seventh degree of the major scale does not change to mixolydian.

Students can often be led into changing the mode of a song without verbal preparation. While the teacher provides a chordal accompaniment, students may sing silently through a song, then sing aloud with the accompaniment. Figure 3.5 includes three primary chords for accompanying in each mode. Note that only major and minor have all three chords in common. When melodies are changed from major or minor to one of the other modes, chordal accompaniments must be changed also for the new mode.

A teaching technique for changing a song that was first learned in major to minor is to preface the song with a minor arpeggio or i-V7-i chordal progression and begin singing the song. Avoid verbal explanations and notational or theoretical information at this point. After singing through the song in the new mode, give students an appropriate starting pitch and any new fingerings necessary to perform the song on their instruments.

It is also necessary and desirable to change major and minor melodies into other modes when using notation. When students have aural readiness for modes and are reading notation accurately, it is possible to change to parallel modes of notated melodies by altering key signatures. The melody is performed in a new mode by reading the same notes with a different key signature, and the necessary range for an instrument is not changed. Minor songs may be changed to dorian by adding one sharp or removing one flat from the minor key signature. Minor songs may be changed to phrygian by adding one flat or removing one sharp. Major songs change to mixolydian by adding a flat or removing a sharp, and to lydian by adding a sharp or removing a flat. Major songs change to minor by adding three flats or removing three sharps.

Remember that when deciding which mode to switch to, the characteristic tones of the new mode must be in the melodic line in order for the mode to be recognizable. Also, these changes are only possible melodically because underlying chordal accompaniments are different when switching major or minor songs to other modes. Accompaniments for the changed songs would need to be altered with some different chords and cadences (see Figure 3.5).

Inference Learning

Generalizing (G) familiar tonal patterns to unfamiliar selections may occur with or without notation. Encourage students to listen for famil-

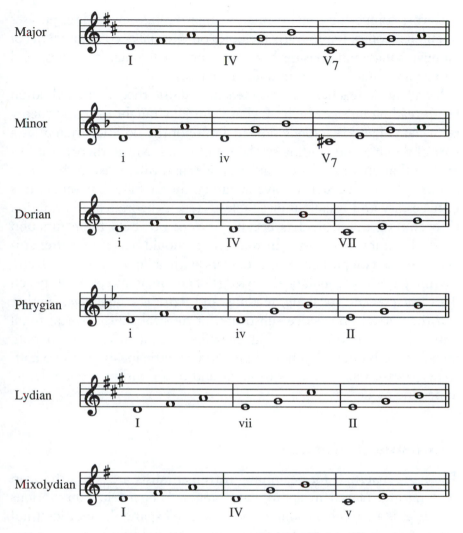

Figure 3.5   KEY OF D CHORD ARPEGGIOS FOR SIX MODES

iar patterns in unfamiliar music, first aurally, later with notation. Sight-reading is an essential activity for learning to recognize familiar patterns in new arrangements. Audiation of tonal patterns will develop as pattern vocabulary grows and is recognized in unfamiliar material.

Creativity and Improvisation (C/I) activities with familiar tonal patterns should be included on a regular basis in lessons and rehearsals. Activities include: composing simple melodies using familiar tonal patterns; composing tonal ostinatos; improvising new ending phrases to familiar songs; improvising melodies on chordal accompaniments of familiar songs; improvising harmony lines to familiar melodies; and performing familiar songs in different modes.

Many music teachers insist on teaching music theory when children begin reading music. Much of what is initially taught as music theory is misnamed and is actually nomenclature of the notation system as a part of naming and reading symbols and terms. Music theory is information that answers why certain practices and rules exist in the music of our culture. In order to have meaning, theory follows practice. It is unnecessary and usually undesirable to teach theoretical information to beginning music readers because it does not help them function musically. If music theory is introduced, it should occur only after students are accomplished music readers with a functional tonal and rhythm pattern vocabulary. Knowledge of grammar and parts of speech does not precede speaking, reading, and writing a language; neither can theoretical knowledge substitute for musical skills. Typical tonal music theory information that may be taught when appropriate includes pitch intervals, chord types, and why the location of two half-steps (always represented with *mi-fa* and *ti-do*) within a scale determines the mode.

Choosing Materials

The basic materials for beginning instrumentalists are songs that can be sung and played in appropriate ranges. Folk music from various countries is an excellent source and means to expand the multicultural content in instrumental music training. Familiar songs from general music classes are particularly useful and appropriate in that students should be able to easily audiate the sounds through their instruments as they develop technique. A list of songs categorized by range appears in Appendix A. These songs may be sung and played without notation, transposed and later read at different pitch levels, performed with switched modes, and used as bases for creative and improvisation activities to develop a sense of tonality and a tonal pattern vocabulary.

Materials should be chosen to teach tonal content objectives. It is helpful for the teacher to develop source files of familiar tunes that work well to teach specific tonal content. The primary goal is to teach the sequence of tonal content and audiation through song literature, not just to teach a collection of songs.

As instrumentalists gain proficiency tonally and technically, the literature emphasis gradually shifts to developing repertoire associated with the particular instrument and ensembles. Students will have necessary tonal skills to sight-read and to generalize to unfamiliar music, and awareness of tonal patterns will become internalized and automatic.

Tonal Objectives

The following list of tonal objectives for instrumentalists incorporates the tonal content with the Gordon learning sequence levels (indicated in parentheses). It is intended as an organizational guide for tonal instruction with beginning instrumentalists regardless of age level. Note that beginning with objective number 6 the content is specific for major and minor tonic function tonal patterns. Similar sequences of objectives 6 through 17 are overlapped simultaneously as indicated. The pacing of the overlapping content must be determined by the teacher after assessment of student achievement. Individual student needs should always be taken into consideration. Recognize also that other similar lists could be constructed with variations in content.

The student will be able to

1. sing/play familiar major and minor songs without notation (A/O)
2. sing/play major and minor tonic arpeggios with syllables but without notation (VA)
3. recognize aurally major and minor resting tones (A/O)
4. label familiar songs as in major or minor mode after hearing or performing without notation (VA)
5. label unfamiliar songs as in major or minor mode after hearing without notation (G)
6. echo-sing/-play major and minor tonic function tonal patterns without syllables or notation (A/O)
7. echo-sing major and minor tonic function tonal patterns with tonal syllables and without notation (VA)
8. sing major and minor tonic function tonal patterns with tonal syllables after hearing patterns performed without notation (VA)

9. recognize aurally major and minor tonic function tonal patterns in familiar songs without notation (PS) (At this point, overlap objectives by simultaneously beginning a content sequence at number 6 with major and minor dominant-seventh function tonal patterns.)

10. recognize aurally major and minor tonic function tonal patterns in unfamiliar songs without notation (G)

11. sing with syllables and play self-created combinations of familiar major and minor tonic function tonal patterns without notation (C/I) (At this point, overlap objectives by simultaneously beginning a content sequence at number 6 with major and minor sub-dominant function tonal patterns)

12. recognize familiar major and minor tonic function tonal patterns in notation (SA)

13. sing with syllables, write, and play notated major and minor tonic function tonal patterns (SA) (At this point, overlap objectives by simultaneously beginning a content sequence at number 6 with supertonic, submediant, mediant function and chromatic tonal patterns)

14. recognize and sing/play familiar major and minor tonic function tonal patterns within notation of familiar songs (CS)

15. recognize and sing/play familiar major and minor tonic function tonal patterns within notation of unfamiliar songs (G)

16. improvise, compose, and perform combinations of familiar written major and minor tonic function tonal patterns (C/I)

17. understand the theoretical basis for harmonic function of major and minor tonic function tonal patterns (TU)

Tonal patterns in dorian, mixolydian, phrygian, and lydian modes may be introduced and taught in the preceding sequence of objectives by making appropriate content changes (see Figure 3.5 for chords). Additional lists of pattern objectives would also require overlapping. It is not desirable or necessary to complete the entire list for one segment of content before beginning a new segment.

The tonal content sequence, which is the basis for the objectives list above, is briefly outlined here in summary:

Sing a repertoire of rote songs in major and minor modes.

Recognize the resting tones of melodies.

Sing and later play arpeggio tune-up patterns in the appropriate mode for any song to be sung or played.

Develop a tonal-pattern vocabulary of

major and harmonic minor

tonic function.

dominant seventh function.

subdominant function.

other chord functions (ii, iii, vi, vii-).

mixolydian and dorian

tonic function.

leading-tone chord function.

subdominant function.

other chord functions.

lydian and phrygian

tonic function.

submediant function.

leading-tone function (lydian), subdominant function (phrygian).

other chord functions.

Most music teacher trainees receive little or no explicit instruction about developing a sense of tonality for themselves or their future students. A frequent consequence is the imposition by school music teachers of the academic aspects of college theory courses on instrumentalists with an emphasis on training the eye rather than the ear. The task of teaching a sense of tonality is not formidable, and teachers should be encouraged to learn and practice through their teaching. A lack of experience and practice with teaching tonal patterns and modes on the part of teachers should not become a limitation placed on their instrumental students. Teaching tonal content through the learning skills sequence can be a rewarding experience for all.

Review Questions

1. What is a sense of tonality?
2. What is the relationship between tonality and keyality?

3. What tonal readiness activity is essential to beginning instrumentalists?
4. On what is singing and playing in tune dependent?
5. Why is it helpful for beginning instrumentalists to work with tunes that include the words?
6. Why should tunes for beginning instrumentalists include the words?
7. What constitutes the Aural/Oral level for a sense of tonality?
8. Why should songs in modes other than major be taught?
9. What are some advantages of using movable *do* syllables to teach tonal patterns?
10. What is a tonal pattern?
11. Why should beginning instrumentalists develop a tonal pattern vocabulary?
12. What basis should be used to select tonal patterns?
13. How are tonal patterns taught with Verbal Association?
14. Why should tonal patterns be practiced in more than one key or pitch level?
15. What are some Partial Synthesis activities for learning tonal patterns?
16. When and how should beginning instrumentalists be introduced to music notation?
17. What is the rationale for interpreting key signatures and naming keys?
18. How should sight-reading be incorporated into instrument instruction?
19. What is the purpose of writing music notation and taking dictation?
20. What are some Composite Synthesis activities for learning tonal patterns?
21. Considering the tonal pattern D $\overline{\text{M}}$ $\overline{\text{S}}$, what would be an appropriate teaching technique at each level of the Gordon learning sequence for beginning instrumentalists?
22. How may tunes be efficiently switched to other modes?
23. When is it appropriate to teach music theory information?
24. What are some criteria for choosing music to teach a sense of tonality?
25. What is the sequence of tonal content discussed in this chapter?

References

DAVIDSON, LYLE S., LARRY SCRIPP, and P. WELSH. (1988). "Happy Birthday": Evidence for conflicts of perceptual knowledge and conceptual understanding. *Journal of Aesthetic Education* 22 (1), 65–74.

DUNLAP, MICHAEL P. (1989). The effects of singing and solmization training on the musical achievement of beginning fifth-grade instrumental students. Ph.D. diss., University of Michigan.

DYKEMA, PETER W., and HANNAH M. CUNDIFF. (1955). *School music handbook.* Boston: C. C. Birchard & Co.

ELLIOTT, CHARLES A. (1972). The effect of vocalization upon the sense of pitch of the students in selected beginning band classes. *Journal of Research in Music Education* 20 (4), 496–500.

FARNSWORTH, PAUL R. (1969). *The social psychology of music*, 2nd ed. Ames, IA: Iowa State University Press.

GORDON, EDWIN E. (1993). *Learning sequences in music.* Chicago: GIA Publications, Inc.

GRUTZMACHER, PATRICIA A. (1987). The effect of tonal-pattern training on the aural perception, reading recognition and melodic sight-reading achievement of first-year instrumental students. *Journal of Research in Music Education* 20 (4), 171–181.

HARRIS, THOMAS JOHN. (1977). An investigation of the effectiveness of an intonation training program upon junior and senior high school wind instrumentalists. Ed.D. diss., University of Illinois.

LUNDIN, ROBERT W. (1985). *An objective psychology of music*, 3rd ed. Malabar, FL: Robert E. Krieger Publishing Co.

MACKNIGHT, CAROL B. (1975). The effects of tonal pattern training on the performance achievement of beginning wind instrumentalists. *Experimental Research in the Psychology of Music: Studies in the Psychology of Music* 10, 53–76.

MCGARRY, ROBERT J. (1967). A teaching experience to measure the extent to which vocalization contributes to the development of selected instrumental music performance skills. Ed.D. diss., New York University.

MEYER, LEONARD. (1956). *Emotion and meaning in music.* Chicago: University of Chicago Press.

———. (1967). *Music, the arts, and ideas.* Chicago: University of Chicago Press.

MURSELL, JAMES L. (1943). *Music in American schools.* New York: Silver Burdett Co.

PHILLIPS, KENNETH. (1992). *Teaching kids to sing.* New York: Schirmer Books.

RADOCY, RUDOLF E., and J. DAVID BOYLE. (1988). *Psychological foundations of musical behavior*, 2nd ed. Springfield, IL: Charles C. Thomas.

SCHLACKS, WILLIAM F. (1981). The effect of vocalization through an interval training program upon the pitch accuracy of high school band students. Ph.D. diss., University of Miami.

SHUTER-DYSON, ROSAMUND, and CLIVE GABRIEL. (1981). *The psychology of musical ability*, 2nd ed. London: Methuen.

SPERTI, JOHN. (1970). Adaptation of certain aspects of the Suzuki Method to the teaching of the clarinet: An experimental investigation testing the comparative effectiveness of two different pedagogical methodologies. Ed.D. diss., New York University.

SUZUKI, SHINICHI. (1969). *Nurtured by love.* New York: Exposition Press.

TAYLOR, JACK A. (1976). Perception of tonality in short melodies. *Journal of Research in Music Education* 24 (4), 197–208.

CHAPTER 4

Teaching Rhythmic Feeling

A student has great difficulty performing accurate rhythms and tempos on the trumpet. The band director notices that the student has little apparent sense of underlying meter feeling and even inserts extra tempo beats occasionally. Why does this student make such slow progress? Is it due to lack of practice, lack of audiation, low rhythm aptitude? What strategies might be used by his teacher to help correct the problem?

Traditional instrumental teaching places great emphasis on rhythmic accuracy as indicated by symbols for proportional note values. Rhythm errors are often the first errors detected by instructors of lessons and rehearsals. Correction of rhythm errors usually involves reference to the mathematics of note durations rather than the underlying rhythmic feeling and flow. As a result, performances often sound mechanical and nonmusical.

Once a true sense of rhythmic feeling is developed, rhythm audiation is possible. This allows instrumentalists to perform in appropriate musical styles as soloists or in ensembles. A vocabulary of rhythm patterns is also a prerequisite for sight-reading and improvisation skills.

Defining Rhythmic Feeling

Musicians and others have created many definitions of rhythm that attempt to be precise and all-encompassing. Most traditional explanations emphasize the duration of musical sounds and then include music notation as examples of proportional note values. Instead of musical sounds taught with rhythmic feeling, the visual and mathematical aspects of rhythm notation become the emphasis of instruction. Many problems result because the symbols used to represent rhythms are often inadequate to express stylistic intent accurately. Rhythm notation becomes most meaningful when rhythmic understandings are represented by the symbols and not derived from the symbols.

The problems of teaching rhythmic feeling are not a recent phenomenon. Mursell and Glenn (1931) note that they

> would regard counting, foot tapping, and the minute study of temporal durations as open to question. As to counting and foot tapping, these are poor ways of generating a sense of rhythm. Instrumental instructors who build wholly upon them ignore the previous rhythmic experience set up in the vocal program. (Of course in some vocal work, no sense of rhythm is built up, and then there is nothing to transfer.) What is wanted is not a sense of one-two-three-four, etc., etc., but a sense of the swing of the music. . . . We may work so hard for mathematically accurate time values, that the pupil thinks of nothing else, and completely loses hold of the rhythmic swing. (p. 311)

Rhythmic flow is the durational organizer of musical sounds. Rhythmic feeling results when the listener or performer responds by perceiving and organizing musical sounds in meaningful patterns without the aid of notation.

Students may be trained to have a sense of rhythmic feeling as well as a sense of tonality. It is possible for almost everyone to improve memory and recognition of rhythms. Rhythms become familiar in music through repeated listening, physical response, and development of a pattern vocabulary. Émile Jaques-Dalcroze ([1921] 1967, 36) stated, "By means of movements of the whole body, we may equip ourselves to realize and perceive rhythms." Rhythmic understanding is aided by anticipation and expectation while listening and performing.

Nearly all Western music has an underlying rhythmic organizer commonly referred to as the beat or pulse. The terms *beat* and *pulse* often have different connotations among musicians and nonmusicians and have limited precision of meaning when referring to rhythmic feeling.

Rhythm is more than a usually obvious "beat." It is helpful to describe and learn rhythmic feeling by working with its various components. To describe the rhythm of a piece of music accurately requires more meaningful terminology with regard to rhythmic feeling. Terminology must also be understandable and usable without confusion by very young children as well as adults. The system of terms for describing rhythmic feeling used throughout this chapter first appeared in Edwin E. Gordon's (1971) *The Psychology of Music Teaching*, in which he defines rhythm as comprising tempo beats, meter beats, and melodic rhythm. Gordon has since altered two of his labels to macro beats (tempo beats) and micro beats (meter beats). This author's preference, based on extensive work with instrumental students of a wide age range, is to retain the original terms.

Tempo beat refers to the recurring underlying feeling in music that acts as the primary rhythmic organizer. Most metronome markings in music refer to the speed or tempo of this beat. Each underlying tempo beat in the tunes of the following song text excerpts is indicated by an *x*.

Yan-kee	Doo-dle	went to	town,
x	x	x	x

Rid-ing	on a	po-	ny
x	x	x	x

Where, oh	where has my	lit-tle dog	gone?
x	x	x	x

Where, oh	where can he	be - - - - - - - -?	
x	x	x	x

Meter beats occur when two or three even subdivisions are super-imposed on tempo beats. Perception of underlying meter beat feeling as tempo beat subdivisions enables a listener to define the rhythmic feeling of music as moving in duple or triple meter. (An exception to this will be discussed later.) As with tempo beats, accurate recognition and feeling for meter is essential for meaningful music listening and performance. The underlying meter beats are indicated with - - or - - - and *x* indicates tempo beats in the following song text examples:

Jin-   gle   bells,   jin-   gle   bells,
  ʾ   ʾ   ʾ   ʾ   ʾ   ʾ   ʾ   ʾ

x   x   x   x

Here we go round   the mul- ber- ry   bush,   the
 ʾ   ʾ   ʾ   ʾ   ʾ   ʾ   ʾ   ʾ   ʾ   ʾ   ʾ   ʾ

x   x   x   x

mul- ber- ry bush   the mul- ber- ry   bush
 ʾ   ʾ   ʾ   ʾ   ʾ   ʾ   ʾ   ʾ   ʾ   ʾ   ʾ   ʾ

x   x   x   x

Melodic rhythm patterns are the last component in the definition of rhythmic feeling. Rhythm patterns are the linear building blocks of rhythmic feeling that interact with tones to produce melody (e.g., the rhythm of song texts). Melodic rhythm patterns are superimposed on underlying tempo beat and meter beat feeling. The rhythmic flow and feeling of a melodic line is dependent on the underlying tempo beat and meter beat feeling. Rhythm patterns may subdivide, elongate, or coincide with underlying tempo beats and meter beats. Rhythm patterns interact with tonal patterns to create melodies but are learned without tonal implications.

Most melodic rhythm patterns may be arbitrarily defined by whatever occurs within one tempo beat. Exceptions occur with patterns that elongate across tempo beats. Most melodies consist of very few rhythm patterns. For example, melodic rhythm patterns are separated in the following song texts by slashes (/):

Over the / river and / through the / woods, to /
grandmother's / house we / go /

Hang down your / head, Tom / Doo-ley,/
Hang down your / head and / cry /

When a functional rhythm pattern vocabulary is developed, music takes on a meaningful dimension of understanding and audiation. A rhythm pattern vocabulary is acquired in the same basic manner that a speaking vocabulary is learned. Sounds are first perceived aurally (A/O) and then practiced orally as labels (words or syllables, VA) for specific meanings. Written symbols are then taught as representations of the sounds (SA). As the vocabulary grows and becomes a means of expression, audiation and the depth of understanding and conceptualization increase.

Rhythm Readiness

A common practice when teaching beginning instrumentalists is to require students to read rhythm notation and "count" accurately while concurrently learning the technical skills of an instrument. For example, asking a beginner to simultaneously hold the instrument in a prescribed manner, form a correct embouchure, blow air through the mouthpiece, read the notation of the exercise, and tap a foot is an invitation to failure. This approach ignores the proper readiness and sequence of small steps necessary to accomplish this complex task. The musical background of typical beginning instrumentalists often includes a repertoire of a few familiar songs and some acquaintance with the names of music symbols. This background experience is important but is inadequate rhythm readiness. Most students come to instrumental training with little or no functional rhythm pattern vocabulary. A sense of rhythm is not acquired by memorizing proportional note values or how many counts a given note value receives; instrumental teachers must provide the appropriate readinesses.

Rhythm readiness begins with kinesthetic response through large-muscle movements to music. This may occur informally to some extent through dance and free movement response while listening to music. Jaques-Dalcroze (1967) recognized the connection of large muscle movement to rhythm response and musical development. His efforts to include movement as a part of musical training have had some influence on general classroom music teaching in this country. The readiness to develop and later read a functional rhythm pattern vocabulary begins with consistent large muscle response to tempo beats. Large-muscle movements such as swaying from side to side, rocking forward and backward, or marching may be readily associated with tempo beat feeling. Accurate meter beat response may then be emphasized as a foundation for a vocabulary of melodic rhythm patterns.

Initial Rhythm Content

If instrumentalists are to perform music with rhythmic accuracy, it is essential that initial content provide appropriate readiness activities and reinforcement. The first task is for students to demonstrate consistent tempo-beat feeling through large muscle movements. Activities that aid consistent tempo-beat response while students are listening to music include: marching, dancing, swaying, rocking as if sitting in a rocking chair, and moving the arms from the shoulders. While sitting, keeping the toe anchored and raising the heel off the floor provides a large-muscle movement of the leg from the hip. Toe-tapping is not a large-muscle movement and is not appropriate as a beginning activity. Toe-tapping may act as a useful rhythm cue only after consistent tempo beat feeling is firmly established.

The next task is for students to demonstrate consistent meter-beat feeling. Movement activities for meter-beat feeling may be included while students demonstrate consistent physical response to tempo beats. In order for a consistent physical response to be associated with duple and triple meter feeling, teach specific movement activities for each meter. Duple meter feeling is associated with pat-clap movements, and triple meter feeling is associated with pat-clap-clap movements. Pats correspond to the tempo beat feeling, and claps correspond with meter-beats. Pat-clap movements should involve the entire arm by moving from the shoulder, the open palms patting on the thighs or clapping together. Movements for meter feeling should be evenly spaced. Pat-claps would occur with the following song text excerpts as indicated by the *p*'s and *c*'s under the words:

Lon - don bridge is   fall- ing   down,
p   c   p   c   p   c   p c

fall- ing   down,   fall- ing   down
p   c   p c   p   c   p   c

Here we   go   round   the   mul - ber -ry   bush, the
p   c   c   p c   c   p   c   c   p c   c

mul - ber - ry   bush,   the   mul -ber - ry   bush,
p   c   c   p   c   c   p   c   c   p

Note that the pat-claps occur with the underlying tempo-beat and meter-beat feeling regardless of location of melodic rhythms as indicated by the text. The physical movement of pat-clapping gives a basis for accuracy of the melodic rhythm patterns through the consistent tempo-beat and meter-beat feeling.

The teacher should choose music with moderate tempo-beat speed that remains constant throughout the melody. Tempo-beats moving in the range of 90 to 110 beats per minute work well for most duple meter songs, and slightly slower speeds work well for triple meter feeling. It is important that the tempo-beat speed allow for comfortable, accurate pat-clap or pat-clap-clap responses. If music moves very slowly, it is difficult to maintain even tempo-beat and meter-beat feeling, and if music moves very rapidly, it becomes difficult to perceive and physically respond to the meter feeling.

When rhythm problems occur in group lessons or rehearsals, it is often helpful to have some students pat tempo-beats only, some pat-clap or pat-clap-clap meter-beat feeling, and others play or sing the melody. Groups may rotate assignments as they gain proficiency in maintaining the rhythmic flow. Tempo-beat movements (pats) and

Flute class with playing and pat-clapping

meter-beat movements (pat-clap or pat-clap-clap) then become a rhythm accompaniment for melodies by emphasizing the underlying rhythmic feeling. The criterion for determining tempo-beat and meter-beat feeling is always the sound and feel of the music, never the notation.

Music does not necessarily have to move with evenly spaced tempo-beats subdivided into twos and threes. Unusual meter feeling occurs when tempo-beats are unevenly spaced and meter beats move in equal durations of twos and threes. Examples are compositions that have a 5 or 7 as the top number of their meter signature. Meter-beat movements should again coincide with the groupings of twos and threes which are determined by the tempo-beat locations. Unusual meters will be discussed in more detail later in this chapter.

Building a Melodic Rhythm Pattern Vocabulary

Melodic rhythm patterns are small units of the linear movement of melody. The patterns follow the rhythm of the words in songs with texts. Secure tempo-beat and meter-beat feelings are the foundations on which accurate melodic rhythm patterns are performed. Most of the time, melodic rhythm patterns may be limited to what occurs within one tempo beat. Rhythm patterns include more than one tempo beat whenever melodic pitches are held (elongated) across the underlying tempo-beat feeling. The following song text examples have the melodic rhythm patterns separated by slashes, the meter-beat feeling indicated with *p c* or *p c c*, and the tempo beats indicated by *x*:

```
Koo-ka  bur-ra /  sits    on the/  old       gum /  tree /
p         c       p     c        p       c      p    c
x                 x               x              x
```

```
O-   ver   the / riv-  er   and/  through  the/  woods   to/
p    c     c    p    c    c       p      c   c     p    c    c
x          x              x             x
```

Again, notice that the rhythm patterns may or may not coincide with the tempo-beat and meter-beat locations. The underlying tempo-beat and meter-beat feeling remain constant regardless of the rhythm patterns in the melody.

Clapping rhythm patterns is a simple way to associate them with physical movement. Clapping should involve arm and hand movement, not
just wrists and hands. Confusion with pat-clap movements for meter-
beat feeling is avoided by associating rhythm pattern clapping with hand
clapping only. Three separate movement associations are then available
for rhythm practice with tempo beats (pats), meter beats (pat-clap or
pat-clap-clap), and melodic rhythm patterns (clapping). Groups of students may be subdivided and assigned the three different movements to
be performed simultaneously while others play instruments.

Using Rhythm Syllables

Rhythm syllables are frequently used in traditional instrumental teaching, the most common ones being "1-e-and-a" and "1-and-a." Others
include "1-la-li," "1-ta-te-ta," and "ta-a-a." There are many inconsistencies in the use and associations of these systems, but the most seri-
ous problem is that almost without exception, the systems are taught
concurrently with notation as a means of learning proportional note
values. Rhythm syllables are traditionally used to teach notation visually, not rhythmic feeling or aural rhythm patterns. Inefficiency and
confusion result from attempts to derive musical meaning *from* notation rather than to bring musical meaning *to* notation.

In order to learn a vocabulary of rhythm patterns efficiently and
effectively, a system of verbal association with the sound of patterns is
necessary. Using syllables to label rhythm sounds is convenient and
practical. A syllable system should be monosyllabic and easy to speak
or chant by very young children as well as adults. No syllables should
duplicate those used in tonal patterns, and different but related syllables should be used for duple, triple, and unusual meters. Rhythm syllables should not be confused with articulation or tonguing syllables
used with wind instruments. Syllables should *never* be introduced concurrently with notation; they are intended for initial use only with pattern sounds. Syllables should *not* be chanted melodically throughout
entire tunes; again, they are intended for use only with pattern sounds.
Clear associations with feeling and sound must be established if
rhythm syllables are to have a meaningful purpose.

A rhythm syllable system that meets all of the above stated criteria was adapted by Gordon (1971) from a system authored by McHose and Tibbs (1945). Tempo-beat locations within patterns are labeled with the numbers 1 or 2 in duple and triple meters. Meter-beat locations for duple feeling are given the syllable ne ("nay"), and for triple feeling na ("nah") ni ("nee"). All further subdivisions receive the syllable ta ("tah"). Unusual meter receives different but related syllables with be ("bay") for duple feeling and ba ("bah") bi ("bee") for triple feeling subdivisions of tempo beats. Tempo beats in unusual meters are assigned the syllable du ("doo") rather than numbers to avoid confusion when grouped unevenly.

The following examples illustrate how the rhythm syllables superimpose on the underlying tempo and meter beat feeling:

Duple Meter

1	ta	ne	ta	2	ta	ne	ta
1		ne		2		ne	
1				2			
p		c		p		c	

Triple Meter

1	ta	na	ta	ni	ta	2	ta	na	ta	ni	ta
1		na		ni		2		na		ni	
1						2					
p		c		c		p		c		c	

Unusual Meter (e.g., 5 as upper number of meter signature)

du	ta	be	ta	du	ta	ba	ta	bi	ta
du		be		du		ba		bi	
du				du					
p		c		p		c		c	

or

du	ta	ba	ta	bi	ta	du	ta	be	ta
du		ba		bi		du		be	
du						du			
p		c		c		p		c	

This rhythm syllable system has received some research interest—Dittemore (1970), DeYarman (1975), and Palmer (1976)—and considerable success in field development experiences with music teachers throughout the country. Gordon (1993) currently prefers a variation of the syllables for duple (*du de*) and triple (*du da di*) feeling. The vowels are the same but the consonants are changed to *d*'s. Numbers on all tempo beats are replaced with the syllable *du*. This variation of syllables still meets the criteria stated above for choosing rhythm syllables for verbal assocation. This author prefers the use of numbers on tempo beats in duple and triple meter feeling as a helpful reference label before and after notation is introduced; students can operate efficiently with them.

Rhythm syllables, meter-beat feeling, and tempo-beat feeling are indicated under the following patterns, which are separated by slashes in these song text examples:

```
Koo-ka- bur-ra / sits    on the/old        gum / tree /
1    ta ne ta  2     ne ta 1        ne     2
p       c       p    c      p       c      p       c
x               x           x              x
```

```
O-  ver the/riv- er    and/through the/ woods    to/
1    na  ni 2   na   ni  1     ni 2           ni
p   c   c  p   c    c   p c   c   p   c    c
x          x           x           x
```

```
Lon-  don /      bridge    is /  fall-  ing / down, /
1     ne        2         ne   1    ne   2
p     c         p          c    p   c    p    c
x               x              x         x
```

```
Here  we   go /  round     the / mul- ber- ry /  bush,      the/
1     na   ni  2           ni  1   na   ni  2           ni
p     c    c   p    c    c  p   c    c   p    c    c
x               x              x              x
```

```
We   wish  you a   mer-ry/ Christ-   mas, we /
ni    1    na ta  ni  ta 2        na  ni
c    p     c      c     p         c   c
     x                  x
```

Notice that the rhythm syllables fit with the rhythm of the words. Some of the patterns coincide with underlying tempo- and meter-beat feeling; others further subdivide the meter- or tempo-beat feeling.

Syllables are associated with the *sound* and *feel* of melodic rhythm patterns. Rhythm verbal association does *not* mean associating syllables with specific note values (e.g., ta equals a quarter note), nor does it mean chanting or counting aloud the underlying subdivisions of the tempo beats while reading and clapping the melodic rhythms.

More Rhythm Pattern Teaching Techniques

It becomes obvious that most melodies found in beginning and intermediate instrumental music consist of very few rhythm patterns. Furthermore, these same few rhythm patterns are used again and again and are repeated in different combinations throughout music of the western world. Figures 4.1 and 4.2 contain notation for eleven duple and fifteen triple meter rhythm patterns. The first nine duple patterns and the first four triple patterns account for nearly all beginning song literature found in instrumental method books. By learning to recognize aurally, to associate syllables, to read, and to write a vocabulary of relatively few rhythm patterns, students are able to perform with rhythmic feeling and accuracy.

After consistent tempo- and meter-beat feeling is demonstrated, students should begin to work aurally with patterns. The first patterns taught should be ones that coincide with the tempo- and meter-beat feelings in duple and triple (patterns D1, D2, T1, and T2 in Figures 4.1 and 4.2). Patterns should be clapped, chanted, and played. Rhythm patterns should relate to familiar tunes that are sung and played so their recognition and use is continually reinforced.

The sequence of learning rhythm begins with physical response to tempo-beat and meter-beat feeling in duple and triple. Acquiring a pattern vocabulary begins with echo-clapping of tempo and meter beat patterns without syllables or notation (A/O). Echo-clapping and dialogue activities with a few patterns at a time establish familiarity with the sound and feeling of the rhythms. When doing pattern activities, students may realize the underlying tempo-beat feeling by rocking slightly forward and back from the hips for duple meter and by swaying slightly from side to side for triple meter. In groups of students, a few may be assigned tempo-beat movements, a few meter-beat movements, and others clap patterns. Pitches may be assigned to echo-play rhythm patterns on instruments.

Figure 4.1   MELODIC RHYTHM PATTERNS FOR DUPLE (D)
METER FEELING

Rhythm syllables should be added when facility for echo-clapping a few patterns is achieved. Association of rhythm syllables (VA) to patterns is easily accomplished by echo-chanting and dialogue activities. While maintaining a consistent tempo-beat feeling, the teacher chants a pattern and students immediately repeat it in tempo. Chanted syllable responses should always be within the given tempo. The complexity of the task increases when the teacher only claps the patterns and students must answer in rhythm by chanting the correct syllables.

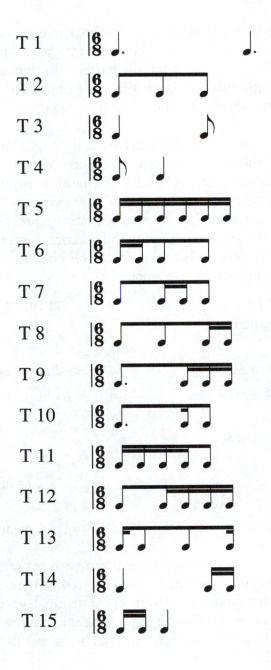

Figure 4.2   MELODIC RHYTHM PATTERNS FOR TRIPLE (T)
METER FEELING

Verbal association has taken place when students can consistently demonstrate the correct syllable chanting for clapped patterns, and at that point they are ready to see the patterns in notation. Additional patterns are introduced through the same process of echo-clapping. Again, patterns should be chosen from familiar songs in duple and triple meter.

Tempo beats are generally perceived and grouped aurally in pairs, regardless of the meter feeling. Therefore, the process of echo-chanting beginning patterns is aided by chanting patterns across pairs of tempo beats. By combining patterns over two pairs of tempo beats, a rhythmic phrase is implied. Clapping, chanting, and playing patterns in groups of four tempo beats is a useful practice. Patterns may first be repeated for each tempo beat and then later changed on each tempo beat to add complexity. For example:

TEACHER					*STUDENT*			
(duple patterns)								
1	2	1	2		1	2	1	2
1 ne	2 ne	1 ne	2		1 ne	2 ne	1 ne 2	
1	2 ne	1 ne	2		1	2 ne	1 ne 2	

(triple patterns)								
1	2	1	2		1	2	1	2
1	2 na ni	1 na ni	2		1	2 na ni	1 na ni	2
1 na ni 2		1 na ni	2		1 na ni	2	1 na ni	2
1 na ni 2 na ni 1					1 na ni	2 na ni	1	

More than one repetition may be given each set of patterns. New patterns are readily assimilated when inserted as the second or third tempo beat in the groupings of four. The difficulty level of a set of four patterns increases when a pattern including subdivisions is used on the fourth tempo beat. For example, the following sets of patterns each may be echoed:

1	ne	2	ta	ne	ta	1		ne	2	ta	ne	ta
1	ne	2		ne		1	ta	ne	2	ta	ne
1	ne	2		ne	ta	1		ne	ta	2

1	na	ni	2	ta	na	ta	ni	ta	1	na		ni		2
1	na	ni	2		na	ta	ni	ta	1	na	ta	ni	ta	2
1	na	ni	2				ni	ta	1		ta	ni		2

Figures 4.3 and 4.4 list the correct syllables for the patterns appearing in Figures 4.1 and 4.2. It is critical for the reader to understand that the rhythm syllables should never be introduced to students in conjunction with notation. It is done here only because of the limitations of the printed word in describing musical sounds. *Syllables are intended for use only with the sound and feel of the rhythm patterns.* Rhythm syllables should not associate with specific note values. The patterns in Figures 4.1 and 4.2 are one representation of the sounds. Different symbols are used later to represent the familiar sounds of the same patterns.

As a pattern vocabulary with syllable associations is acquired, and before notation is introduced, it is important to allow opportunities for students to utilize their vocabulary. Activities might include aurally recognizing where certain patterns occur in familiar and unfamiliar songs (PS); listing familiar songs that begin with or contain a particular pattern or series of patterns (PS); counting how many times a pattern occurs within a song (PS); substituting or rearranging patterns in familiar tunes (C/I); stringing familiar patterns together while playing a given pitch (C/I); playing strings of patterns as rhythm rounds on given pitches with others (C/I); and improvising rhythmic variations on familiar tunes (C/I).

Duple and triple songs should be taught concurrently so comparison of meter feeling is possible. Very few triple meter songs are found in beginning instrumental music books, and they are often not taught with triple meter feeling. Method books can often be supplemented with triple meter folk songs or popular tunes. A list of triple meter songs appears in Appendix B.

Switching Meters

A valuable technique for teaching a sense of meter is to switch the meter feeling of familiar songs. This may be done with or without notation. The tempo-beat feeling must remain in the same location when switching the meter of a song. Meters of songs are readily switched by first establishing the correct physical movement for the new meter. For example, close your eyes and audiate the first phrase of "Yankee

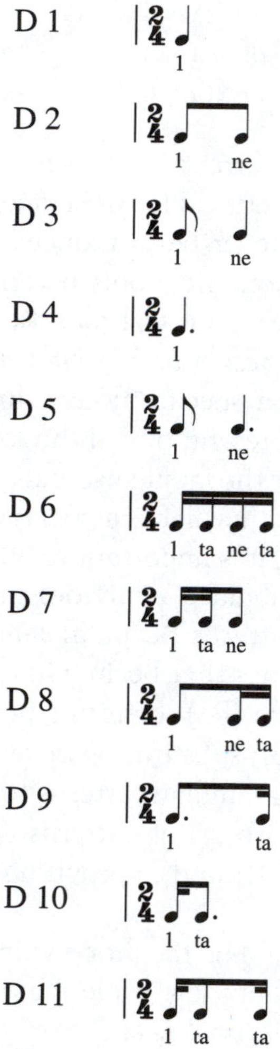

D 1 | 2/4 ♩   ♩
           1   2

D 2 | 2/4 ♫
           1 ne

D 3 | 2/4 ♪ ♩   ♪
           1 ne   ne

D 4 | 2/4 ♩.   ♪
           1   ne

D 5 | 2/4 ♪ ♩.
           1 ne

D 6 | 2/4 ♬♬
           1 ta ne ta

D 7 | 2/4 ♫♪
           1 ta ne

D 8 | 2/4 ♪♫
           1 ne ta

D 9 | 2/4 ♩. ♪
           1   ta

D 10 | 2/4 ♫♩.
           1 ta

D 11 | 2/4 ♫♪
           1 ta ta

Figure 4.3   MELODIC RHYTHM PATTERNS WITH SYLLABLES
             FOR DUPLE (D) METER FEELING

Doodle" with the following duple syllables and pat-claps:

Yan-	kee	Doo-	dle	went	to	town,
1	ne	2	ne	1	ne	2
p	c	p	c	p	c	p	c

It is easily shifted to triple feeling by audiating with the triple syllables
and pat-clap-claps:

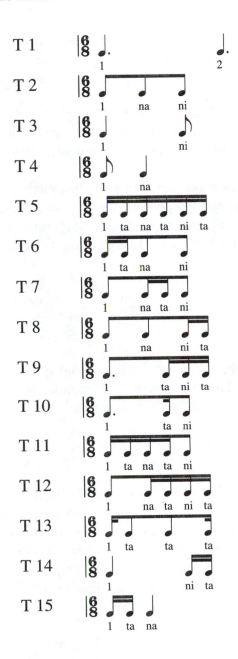

Figure 4.4   MELODIC RHYTHM PATTERNS WITH SYLLABLES
FOR TRIPLE (T) METER FEELING

Yan-	kee	Doo-	dle	went	to	town,	
1	ni	2	ni	1	ni	2	
p c c			p c c		p c c	p	c	c

Duple and triple meter patterns may be mixed together in the same exercise or song—such as triplets in a basically duple meter piece. Combined meter patterns may only occur with evenly spaced tempo-beat feeling.

Songs in duple or triple meter may also be switched to unusual meter feeling by keeping the tempo beats in the same location. The tempo beats become unevenly spaced because the meter beats must be evenly spaced across all groupings. "Yankee Doodle" could be started as follows:

Yan-	kee	Doo-	dle	went	to	town,	
du	bi	du	be	du	bi	du	
p c c		p	c	p c	c	p	c

Students may make different decisions about how the pattern sounds should be arranged in a new meter. For example, the duple feeling pattern could be changed to triple feeling as follows:

1	ne ta	becomes	1	na ni		or	1	ta ni
p	c		p	c c			p	c c

There is no absolutely "correct" version. To facilitate meter switching by groups of instrumentalists, assign a few individuals the physical movements for the tempo beats and a few the movements for meter beats while others perform with instruments. A secure sense of meter may be developed by regularly singing and playing familiar tunes in different meter feelings. This technique compensates for the lack of published materials in other than duple meter.

Dialogue Techniques

As with tonal patterns, dialogue techniques are also especially effective as measurement techniques with rhythm patterns where many students can individually demonstrate skill and knowledge in brief periods of time. Diagnosis of student achievement levels and skills is facilitated. For example, during a dialogue activity, the teacher discovers that a particular student can provide the correct rhythm syllables (VA) for a given clapped pattern but is unable to read the pattern. The student may recognize the written symbols but cannot read and perform them accurately in rhythm. This indicates a need for more practice with the syllables (VA) before further reading of the pattern.

The examples described below are for rhythm pattern dialogues. The statements (S) may be provided by the teacher or by a student leader. It is recommended that patterns be restricted to four tempo beats for each statement and response. Three forms of response (R) are included—clapping, chanting (with correct rhythm syllables), or playing.

1. (S) Clap patterns (Aural/Oral recall or creativity)
    (R) Clap/play different patterns (A/O recall or creativity)
2. (S) Clap patterns (A/O recall or creativity)
    (R) Chant same patterns (VA)
3. (S) Chant patterns (VA creativity—unless pattern is read)
    (R) Clap/play different patterns (A/O creativity)
4. (S) Chant patterns (VA creativity or SA if read)
    (R) Chant different patterns (VA creativity)

The task difficulty of the preceding rhythm dialogues may be increased by 1) alternating duple with triple meter statement and responses; 2) using unusal meter patterns; 3) alternating duple or triple meter with unusual meter statements and responses; 4) using different patterns on each of the four tempo beats within a statement and response, thus increasing the memory task; 5) increasing the number of sounds per pattern; 6) including patterns with ties and elongations across tempo beats; and 7) stressing less familiar or more recently learned patterns. The teacher must take care that difficulty levels do not frustrate students.

Reading Rhythmic Notation

As previously mentioned, notation for any given rhythm patterns may be introduced when correct syllables are consistently chanted with the sound of the patterns. Rhythm notation then represents the familiar aural vocabulary rather than a mathematical system of note values and proportions. Use note value names initially as descriptive labels, not music theory information. Knowledge of note-value proportionalities and fractionalizations is unnecessary. Familiar songs may be performed that are composed of familiar patterns.

An effective technique for associating symbols with patterns is to use a series of flash cards. After students demonstrate that they can chant correct syllables for sounded patterns, show them the same patterns on flash cards. No explanation of the notation is necessary beyond that this is the "picture" of the sounds . . . (chant the pattern). Six cards may be constructed from eight-by-thirty-inch tagboard. The flash cards should be large enough to be seen by groups. Each card should contain the appropriate meter signature and patterns to complete four tempo beats. Here are examples for three duple and three triple meter cards:

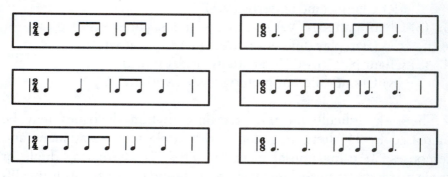

Separate shorter cards should then be constructed for each of the tempo beat patterns displayed in Figures 4.1 and 4.2. The short cards should be just wide enough to cover the space of one tempo beat on the long cards. It is now possible for the teacher or students to arrange many permutations of patterns over the duration of four tempo beats. The patterns on the cards may be clapped, chanted, and/or performed on given pitches. After students are familiar with the patterns written in two-quarter and six-eighth, prepare flash cards with the same pattern sounds and syllables written in two-half and three-quarter. Now the two notations for the same sounds may be visually compared with ease. Additional cards may be constructed for patterns in unusual meter signatures such as five-eighth or seven-eighth. Patterns on cards should always be chanted or performed in an established tempo.

Teacher using rhythm flashcards with clarinet class

Additional teaching techniques with rhythm flash cards are as follows:

Ask students to arrange the large cards and the short cards in various orders for performance. Blackboard trays or music stands may be used as holders.

Create a rhythm ostinato by having one or more students repeat one card while others perform a series of cards.

Create a rhythm round by assigning students to begin on different tempo beat locations simultaneously and perform the patterns through to each starting point.

Associating symbols with rhythm patterns (SA) is also expedited through regular written assignments. The mechanics of music notation are first learned by careful copying of familiar tunes and flash card patterns. Home assignments might include copying a portion of the lesson materials, writing familiar patterns in new arrangements, writing the rhythm notation of popular songs, or composing percussion ensembles from multiple lines of rhythm patterns. Students should be expected to perform their own and each other's written work.

Brief dictation tests of familiar rhythm patterns should be a regular part of most lessons once notation is introduced. Dictation of familiar rhythm patterns begins with the instructor and students establishing the tempo-beat and meter-beat feeling with pat-claps. Students should chant the rhythm syllables aloud or silently for the sounded patterns and then write the correct notation. They may then perform their notation with their instruments or by clapping. Patterns for dictation should be taken only from their vocabulary of familiar ones with verbal association. The first content sequence might include D1, D2, D6, D7, D8, D9, and D11 from Figure 4.1 above. Initial exercises may include only two patterns within four tempo beats and then expand to the others as students demonstrate writing facility. Dictation is a primary technique to determine the rhythm audiation level of students.

As with reading pitch notation after associating sounds with movable *do* syllables, rhythm syllables are the verbal associations with familiar rhythm patterns now represented by symbols. Rhythm syllables are intended for use with patterns only; tunes and exercises should not be chanted through with syllables. Rhythm syllables should be taught by chanting in tempo and not associated with pitch or melody. The goal is to develop audiation so students hear and feel what they see. Syllable use eventually is internalized and need only be thought about with new or troublesome patterns.

Teachers often neglect Composite Synthesis activities when working with rhythm notation, so here is a sampling of possible student tasks:

1. Visually recognize familiar patterns in familiar songs in notation and circle them.
2. Visually count how many times a given pattern occurs in a familiar song.
3. Recognize familiar patterns in familiar songs while singing or playing them from notation.
4. Recognize the meter of a familiar song that contains familiar patterns while listening, singing, or playing with notation.
5. Chain familiar patterns together through singing or playing to reconstruct a familiar song with notation.
6. Name, sing, or play songs that contain a given pattern with notation.

Also, as in the previous chapter, here is a summary example with a list of activities that follow the Gordon learning skills sequence in teaching a rhythm pattern through the Discrimination level of Composite Synthesis. Given the *sound* of (specify a rhythm pattern from Figure 4.1 or 4.2), students will

- echo-clap the pattern (A/O)
- echo-chant the pattern using rhythm syllables (VA)
- hear the pattern when clapped or tapped and respond by chanting the correct rhythm syllables (VA)
- echo-perform the pattern with an instrument on one pitch (VA)
- name a familiar song that contains the pattern (PS)

Given the notation of (specify a rhythm pattern), students will

- chant the pattern using rhythm syllables (SA)
- perform the pattern with an instrument on one pitch (SA)
- locate the pattern within the notation of a familiar song (CS)

Meter Signatures

When interpreting meter signatures, the emphasis should be on what information can be given about rhythmic feeling. The traditional explanation of meter signatures is that the top number refers to how many beats per measure and the lower number refers to the note value that receives one beat. In effect, this is a half-truth. The traditional definition ignores the fact that duple and triple meter signatures indicate different kinds of "beats." If students were knowledgeable about the inconsistencies of the definition, the question would occur immediately, "What kind of beats?" More accurate and meaningful definitions are: duple meter signatures—top numbers are equal to the number of *tempo beats* per measure, lower numbers refer to the note value equal to one *tempo beat*; triple and unusual meter signatures—top numbers are equal to the number of *meter beats* per measure, lower numbers refer to the note value equal to one *meter beat*. Students should memorize that top numbers 2 or 4 indicate duple meter feeling; 3, 6, and sometimes 9 or 12 indicate triple meter feeling; 5, 7, 11, and sometimes 9 indicate unusual meter feeling.

Examples of meter signature definitions that provide rhythmic feeling information are listed in Table 4.1. Notice how each definition provides information about rhythmic feeling rather than just note values.

All patterns with duple feeling are first introduced with two-quarter meter signatures, and all patterns with triple feeling appear first with six-eighth meter signatures. Initially, it is not sensible or practical to expect instrumental beginners to associate many different symbols with each rhythm feeling concept. In two-quarter meter signature, the tempo beat is visually associated with a quarter note value, and in six-eighth meter signature, the tempo beat is visually associated with the dotted quarter note. The meter beat is associated with the eighth note value in both meter signatures. In these two meter signatures, patterns that coincide with the underlying meter feeling always appear with beamed notation (♫ and ♬). This aids visual separation of patterns by tempo beats.

The emphasis in teaching notation is that note values must always represent familiar patterns recognized aurally by their syllable associations. After patterns are known and recognized in two-quarter and six-eighth meter signatures, the same familiar patterns should be symbolically associated with note values in other meter signatures.

The first step when changing to new meter signatures is to move to meter signatures which have new upper numbers but the same lower numbers: four-quarter for duple feeling and three-eighth for triple feeling. The net result is a change in the number of bar lines. The note values and syllables are the same as before. For example:

Table 4.1

METER SIGNATURE EXPLANATIONS

DUPLE METER SIGNATURES

2 = two tempo beats per measure
4 = a quarter note equals a tempo beat

4 = four tempo beats per measure
4 = a quarter note equals a tempo beat

2 = two tempo beats per measure
2 = a half note equals a tempo beat

2 = two tempo beats per measure
8 = an eighth note equals a tempo beat

TRIPLE METER SIGNATURES

6 = six meter beats per measure
8 = an eighth note equals a meter beat

3 = three meter beats per measure
8 = an eighth note equals a meter beat

3 = three meter beats per measure
4 = a quarter note equals a meter beat

6 = six meter beats per measure
4 = a quarter note equals a meter beat

UNUSUAL METER SIGNATURES

5 = five meter beats per measure
8 = an eighth note equals a meter beat

5 = five meter beats per measure
4 = a quarter note equals a meter beat

7 = seven meter beats per measure
8 = an eighth note equals a meter beat

7 = seven meter beats per measure
4 = a quarter note equals a meter beat

Note that in the duple example, every other bar line is removed, and in the triple example, twice as many bar lines are needed when the meter signature is changed. In this step, the notation of the patterns does not change, but the number of tempo beats per measure does change. In the duple example, a measure of four-quarter is formed by removing the bar line between two measures of two-quarter. It must be understood that the sound of the patterns remains constant regardless of the number of bar lines. When moving from two to four tempo beats per measure, it is not necessary to count them 1 - 2 - 3 - 4. Most students will still see and count the patterns as 1 - 2 - 1 - 2 in each measure regardless of the change in bar lines. Likewise, when moving from six meter beats (two tempo beats) to three meter beats (one tempo beat) per measure, it is not necessary to count each measure as 1 - 1 - 1 - 1. Students tend to group tempo beats in pairs across bar lines as 1 - 2 - 1 - 2 because they hear the patterns with familiar verbal association. Bar lines only change how music looks, not how it sounds or feels.

The next step is to move familiar rhythm patterns into meter signatures with different lower numbers, which changes the notation for the patterns and results visually in a new written "language" for familiar sounds. It is important to recognize again that the syllables for the pattern sounds remain constant, regardless of the meter signature. For example:

The tempo- and meter-beat feeling is represented by different note values when the lower number of the meter signature is changed. The sounds and the syllables for each pattern remain constant even though the note values are changed. The next duple meter signature to be introduced could be four-eighth, and the next triple meter signature could be six-quarter.

The following example shows how the same set of four melodic rhythm patterns looks when written in four different meter signatures.

Again, remember that the syllables for the pattern sounds remain constant regardless of the meter signature.

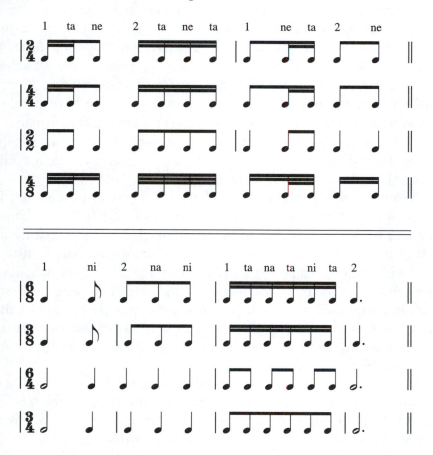

Changing meter signatures and note values for a rhythm pattern is analogous to changing pitch levels for a tonal pattern. The proportions remain constant among note values for any given rhythm pattern written in two different meter signatures. A new set of flash cards may be constructed for each meter signature so familiar patterns may be practiced with differing notation. Notation for familiar tunes may be translated into new meter signature notation and performed.

Most often, insensitive interpretation results from the use of traditional meter signature definitions as mathematical note-value information rather than as an indication of rhythmic feeling. Efficient learning process is ignored when numbers are traditionally used to count tempo beats in duple notation or meter beats in triple notation.

This frequently occurs in beginning method books when students are instructed to count exercises in four-quarter as 1 - 2 - 3 - 4 per measure (usually felt as four tempo beats) and exercises in three-quarter as 1 - 2 - 3 per measure (forcing three tempo beats to be felt per measure rather than three meter beats). *Rhythmic feeling is ignored through visually associating numbers with quarter notes regardless of the underlying meter feeling.* Songs written with three-quarter meter signature are normally felt in one tempo beat per measure and should have numbers associated with tempo beats only. If a song notated in three-quarter is actually felt as three tempo beats per measure, it is no longer triple meter feeling but instead becomes unusual meter with each tempo beat subdivided into duple feeling meter beats.

Another typical example is "slow" six-eighth exercises (counted 1 - 2 - 3 - 4 - 5 - 6) and "fast" six-eighth exercises (counted 1 - 2). Almost without exception, songs written with six-eighth meter signature are felt as two tempo beats per measure. Numbers should only be associated with the two tempo beats and not with the meter beats whenever the tempo is slowed. It is possible to find selections written in six-eighth, six-quarter, or six-half (e.g., many Baroque-period largos) that move very slowly and are felt as six tempo beats per measure; in this case, each measure should be counted 1 - 2 - 3 - 4 - 5 - 6 with ne and ta as syllables for subdivisions.

Avoid having students count the underlying subdivision aloud (e.g., 1 ta ne ta 2 ta ne ta 1 ta ne ta 2 ta ne ta) while clapping the melodic rhythm. This is an inefficient substitute for feeling the underlying meter beats with physical movement. Tempo rushing is a common result. Remember, the verbal association of syllables is with the sound of the melodic rhythm patterns while the underlying tempo beat and meter beat feeling is internalized. Use pat-claps to establish and maintain the meter feeling.

Beginning instrumentalists often perform mechanically and without rhythmic feeling (particularly in triple meter) because of the introduction of counting with the notation and use of the same counting association (numbers) with two distinctly different rhythmic feelings (tempo beats and meter beats). The syllable system and rhythm pattern vocabulary advocated in this chapter eliminate this problem with duple and triple counting.

Another misinterpretation of meter signatures occurs when they are associated with how fast or slow an exercise or song is performed. Some instruction books erroneously imply or instruct that alla breve or *cut* time (¢) is twice as fast as four quarter or *common* time (ȼ). Meter signatures never indicate tempo. Likewise, individual note values never indicate speed—sixteenth notes in one song are not necessarily faster than quarter notes in a different song, etc.—but note values do indicate proportionalities within a given exercise or song. The speed of the tempo beat, regardless of note values, is generally indicated by metronome markings or verbal instructions such as allegro, largo, andante, presto, and so on.

Contemporary music often includes unusual meter signatures (typically with a 5 or 7 as the upper number) where tempo-beat feeling is not equally spaced. In order for beginning instrumentalists to gain familiarity and performance skill with unusual meter feeling, it is advisable to experience simple tunes through singing and playing. It is appropriate to introduce unusual meters after a secure foundation in duple and triple meter feeling is established. Songs should first be sung and accompanied with appropriate pat-claps and pat-clap-claps and then attempted with instruments. Troublesome patterns may be isolated and chanted with syllables. Most beginning instrumental materials contain no unusual meter songs. It is possible and recommended to switch familiar songs learned in duple or triple meter to an unusual meter feeling as explained earlier in this chapter. This adds a new dimension of variation and enjoyment to familiar tunes.

Teaching Patterns with Rests

Rests may be systematically introduced when students can demonstrate consistent tempo-beat and meter-beat feeling and have acquired a basic vocabulary of rhythm patterns with verbal association. Portions of silence may be incorporated into familiar patterns by echoing patterns and substituting a specified physical movement (such as both hands with palms up) for the rest instead of the corresponding rhythm syllable. Rhythm syllables are not sounded for rests. Rests may be explained as taking the place of certain portions of the sound in familiar patterns or substituting silence for certain sounds.

Rests are particularly easy to introduce in notation. Flash cards for each of the commonly used rest symbols may be placed over corresponding note values on rhythm pattern flash cards. Students should then practice chanting and performing the rhythm patterns from flash cards with rests included. Again, rhythm syllables should not be chanted aloud during rests. It is often helpful to accompany patterns that include rests with underlying tempo-beat and/or meter-beat physical movements.

Teaching Dotted Notation

Instrumental music teachers who begin instrument instruction concurrent with notation and without rhythm readiness and vocabulary often delay teaching dotted notation for a number of months. Students are then introduced to dotted notation through explanations of note proportionalities (a dotted quarter note equals three eighth notes, etc.) without relation to underlying rhythmic feeling. Consequently, most students have great difficulty in performing dotted notation accurately.

Conversely, if melodic rhythm patterns are taught initially with syllable associations and no notation, dotted note patterns become no more difficult to learn than any other patterns. Such patterns as D4, D5, D9, and D10 in Figure 4.1 may be introduced in notation whenever students can demonstrate syllable associations for the sound of the patterns. Performance accuracy should always be stressed; teachers should incorporate the movements for the underlying tempo-beat and meter-beat feeling whenever performance problems occur. After notation is introduced, it is sometimes helpful to point out how tempo-beat or meter-beat notation is tied together and sounded as a dotted note. Students can then perform the patterns with rhythmic feeling.

Summary of Some Rhythm Teaching Points

The following points are listed as a quick digest of some of the main points with regard to teaching rhythm patterns as displayed in Figures 4.1 and 4.2:

- Tempo beats are represented with numbers in duple and triple meter feeling and with *du* in unusual meter feeling; subdivisions are represented with syllables
- Numbers and syllables are always associated initially with the sound of the patterns, then the notation

- Rests may be substituted for any given sounds (notes) in a pattern
- Ties may be used to elongate patterns over tempo beats
- Portions of patterns may be used as pick-up notes
- Always chant, clap, or perform patterns in a consistent tempo
- Associate rocking back and forth and pat-clapping with duple meter feeling, and swaying from side to side and pat-clap-clapping with triple meter feeling
- Translate patterns notationally (sound and syllables remain the same) through this sequence of duple meter signatures:

$$\frac{2}{4}, \quad \frac{4}{4}, \quad \frac{2}{2}, \quad \frac{4}{2}, \quad \frac{2}{8}, \quad \frac{4}{8}$$

and this sequence of triple meter signatures:

$$\frac{6}{8}, \quad \frac{3}{8}, \quad \frac{3}{4}, \quad \frac{6}{4}$$

Meter and Conducting Patterns

Conductors of instrumental ensembles often give confusing information to performers when it is unclear whether the basic beat pattern is coinciding with tempo-beat or meter-beat feeling. Rhythmic feeling and flow is reinforced when students understand whether the underlying tempo-beat or meter-beat feeling is conveyed by the conductor.

Rhythmic feeling should be conveyed visually through conducting patterns in group rehearsals and performances. It is the conductor's responsibility to correlate the beat pattern with the underlying feeling and inform the performers of the desired effect. Confusion may occur when the same beat patterns are used indiscriminately to indicate tempo-beat feeling and meter-beat feeling.

Three basic beat patterns are used for conducting rhythmic feeling:

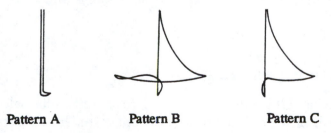

Pattern A   Pattern B   Pattern C

Whenever Pattern A is used, it indicates two tempo beats per measure and is normally used with music written with meter signatures of two-quarter, two-half, two-eighth, and six-eighth. It is also used for meter signatures with 5 as the upper number to indicate the two uneven tempo beats. Many songs are written with a 4 as the upper meter signature number but are actually felt as two tempo beats per measure as in alla breve. Pattern A is appropriate for any music that is felt in two tempo beats per measure, regardless of the meter signature. Note that this same beat pattern may be used for music in duple, triple, or unusual meter feeling. The music will be visually grouped in two tempo beats per measure according to whatever note values are assigned the tempo-beat feeling.

Pattern B is used to indicate four tempo beats per measure. It is normally employed with music written in four-quarter, four-half, four-eighth, and twelve-eighth. It is also used with nine-eighth when it represents unusual meter with four tempo beats per measure. It is also possible (although usually confusing) to use Pattern B to indicate duple meter-beat feeling in music written with two tempo beats per measure. Again, notice that the same beat pattern may be used for music in duple, triple, or unusual meter feeling. Visual representation of the number of tempo beats felt per measure determines the correct beat pattern.

Pattern C is commonly used and is appropriate for indicating three meter beats per measure in three-half, three-quarter, and three-eighth whenever the music is felt with one tempo beat per measure. Music written with three as the top meter signature number and felt as one tempo beat per measure can also be conducted with rhythmic flow by using Pattern A for every two measures. Pattern C may also be used to indicate three tempo beats per measure in music with meter signatures of three-half, three-quarter, three-eighth, and nine-eighth. Special care must be taken when using Pattern C always to inform the performers whether tempo- or meter-beat feeling is indicated by the beat pattern.

Inference Learning

Generalizing (G) familiar rhythm patterns to unfamiliar selections may occur with or without notation. Encourage students to listen for patterns they know in unfamiliar music. Sight-reading material is essential for learning to recognize familiar patterns in new arrangements. Audiation of rhythm patterns will develop as pattern vocabulary grows and is recognized in unfamiliar material.

Creativity and Improvisation. Activities with familiar rhythm patterns should be included on a regular basis in lessons and rehearsals. Activities include changing the melodic rhythm of a familiar tune by performing it with different rhythms; making up simple melodies with a variety of rhythm patterns; composing percussion ensembles; composing percussion accompaniments to melodies; and composing rhythm rounds and ostinatos.

Little has been said so far concerning the teaching of rhythm theory (TU) and notation. This was intentional. Why and how the rhythm system operates as it does becomes meaningful only after functional use. Many teachers insist that students learn proportional note values before performing from notation. Mathematical relationships among note durations are examples of theoretical information of little functional use. Theoretical information abounds in many beginning instrumental materials but, as most students demonstrate, it is of minimal value for developing rhythmic feeling. When the emphasis in teaching and learning rhythm begins with sounds and then a syllable pattern vocabulary, rhythm notation and eventually theory are placed in correct perspective. Theory can then function as a musical experience, not just as an academic experience.

Other Considerations

Slowing of tempo for practice and rehearsal is a common technique to correct rhythmic problems and to secure difficult technical passages. Whenever tempos are slowed, it is critical that the underlying tempo- and meter-beat feelings be maintained. If tempo is slowed so much that the meter-beat feeling is changed to tempo-beat feeling, a new rhythmic structure occurs and the melody is no longer felt or performed with the same rhythmic feeling. Tempo should be slowed relatively little for rehearsal purposes of sections only. It is generally best to rehearse entire selections at or near the performance tempo.

It is not uncommon to hear teachers and conductors ask their students, without notation, to "play the scale in quarter notes." In effect, a visual cue is given but without a rhythmic feeling reference. Note values by themselves do not indicate duration or rhythm. Without further definition, the above instruction could mean the quarter note equals a tempo beat, a meter beat, or part of a triplet quarter figure. Meaningful instructions would be to ask students to perform the scale on tempo beats, or on duple meter beats, or on triple meter beats. Now, instead of a confusing visual cue, the directions give specific rhythmic meaning.

Consider the following exercise as a typical example of meter signature practice found in many instrumental method books. It is first intended to be performed with four tempo beats per measure and then with two tempo beats per measure.

This type of exercise may be used but is only appropriate if students understand that 1) the number of tempo beats per measure changes from four to two, 2) the speed of the tempo beats has nothing to do with the meter signature, and 3) new melodic rhythm patterns are formed by the change of meter signatures while keeping the same notation, and this necessitates different rhythm syllables. The counting for the above exercise in four-quarter would be

> 1 2 1 2 / 1 2 1 2 / 1 - 1 - / 1 - 1 - /

or

> 1 2 3 4 / 1 2 3 4 / 1 - 3 - / 1 - 3 - /

The counting for the notation felt in two-half meter signature would be

> 1 ne 2 ne / 1 ne 2 ne / 1 2 / 1 2 /

It should be apparent that the verbal association of the rhythm patterns fits with the sound and feeling of the above example regardless of the meter signature or the note value assigned the tempo beat.

Learning syllables and, later, notation for rhythm patterns may be facilitated with practice exercises placed on cassette tapes. A continuous tempo-beat sound should be supplied by a metronome while patterns are tapped with a contrasting sound. A usable format is: four tempo beats of patterns, four tempo beats of silence for the student to echo-clap the patterns, four tempo beats while teacher chants the patterns with syllables, four tempo beats of silence for the student to echo-chant the patterns, four tempo beats of silence for the student to play the patterns, four tempo beats rest, new set of patterns begins. After correct syllables can be associated with the sounded rhythm patterns, students should be shown all items in written form with two-quarter meter signature for duple patterns and six-eighth meter signature for triple meter patterns. After the written patterns can be accurately chanted with syllables, the taped items should be taken as a dictation test. The next task is to learn the items in two new meter signatures—two-half for duple and three-quarter for triple. The taped items may now be taken in dictation in the new meter signatures. More meter signature changes may follow.

Teaching rhythm notation is often complicated by inconsistent editorial practices, which allow much music to be published that does not accurately represent intended rhythmic feelings. The four-quarter meter signature is particularly abused. It is used correctly when it indicates four tempo beats per measure, but it is frequently used to notate music that is felt with two tempo beats per measure. It is often necessary when practicing with notation for students and/or the teacher first to sing the tune and establish by sound where the tempo-beat and meter-beat feeling occurs. Then, if needed, they can change the meter signature to fit the correct feeling; for example, without altering notation, a four-quarter meter signature may be changed to two-half, which will indicate the feeling of two tempo beats per measure. Conductors should always be aware of these problems, and as Nilo Hovey (1976) points out, "A comparison of meter signature and metronomic indication is always necessary, for they may not agree on the unit of measurement. In this case, the metronome mark should almost always take precedence" (p. 52).

Arrangers of beginning instrumental music often "simplify" familiar tunes by limiting note values to halves, quarters, and eighths, and by avoiding dotted rhythms. Simplified or "watered down" arrangements avoid supposedly difficult rhythms but create more problems than are solved. Students will often perform familiar tunes as they audiate or "know" them rather than how they appear in notation. This demonstrates the importance of audiation before notation rather than sounds extracted from notation. Familiar tunes are best performed as originally learned through singing and listening. Teachers should adjust rhythm notation when necessary to correspond with the version familiar to the students.

Materials

A sense of rhythmic feeling and a rhythm pattern vocabulary are best taught and learned from familiar folk tunes and songs learned in general music classes. Choose materials to correspond with the sequence of patterns to be learned. Written materials should be in the appropriate meter signature sequence. Have students determine tempo beat and meter beat feelings by physical movements and singing if necessary and adjust notation as needed. Student-composed materials may be used extensively. The melodic rhythms of any song may be used as a rhythm round by performing the rhythms on predetermined pitches only, with one or two tempo beat intervals between entries.

It is obvious that the rhythm content of most beginning instrumental method books is designed for teaching symbols of individual note values (whole, half, quarter, eighth, and sixteenth) in order of proportional duration rather than rhythmic feeling and pattern vocabulary. It is undesirable and unnecessary to proceed through method books in the order of the pages. It is always necessary to pick and choose among available materials so that the needs of individual students may be met and a logical rhythm content sequence may be followed.

Rhythm Objectives

The rhythm objectives listed below for instrumentalists incorporate the rhythm content discussed in this chapter with the levels (in parentheses) of the Gordon learning sequence described in Chapter 2. The list is intended as an organizational guide for rhythm instruction for beginning instrumentalists regardless of age level. As with the tonal objectives list, sequences of objectives (7–18) are simultaneously overlapped with pattern content differing. Again, the pacing of the over-lapped sequences must be determined by the teacher and based on assessment of student achievement.

The student will be able to

1. respond to the sound of music with consistent tempo beat movements (A/O)
2. respond to the sound of duple meter music with consistent pat-clapping movements (A/O)
3. respond to the sound of triple meter music with consistent pat-clap-clapping movements (A/O)
4. recognize aurally familiar music without notation as duple or triple meter feeling (A/O)
5. label familiar music as duple or triple meter feeling without notation (VA)
6. label unfamiliar music as duple or triple meter feeling without notation (G)
7. echo-clap/-play duple and triple meter melodic rhythm patterns without notation that coincide with underlying tempo and meter beats (A/O)
8. echo-chant duple and triple tempo- and meter-beat patterns with rhythm syllables and without notation (VA)
9. chant syllables for duple and triple tempo- and meter-beat patterns after hearing patterns sounded without notation (VA)
10. recognize aurally duple and triple tempo- and meter-beat patterns in familiar songs without notation (PS) (At this point, overlap objectives by simultaneously beginning a content sequence at number 7 with duple and triple meter patterns that elongate underlying tempo and meter beats or that subdivide meter beats)
11. recognize aurally duple and triple tempo and meter beat patterns in unfamiliar songs without notation (G)
12. clap/chant/play self-created combinations of familiar duple and triple tempo- and meter-beat patterns without notation (C/I) (At this point, overlap objectives by simultaneously beginning a content sequence at number 7 with unusual meter melodic rhythm patterns that coincide with underlying tempo and meter beats)
13. recognize duple and triple tempo- and meter-beat patterns from notation (SA)

14. clap/chant/play duple and triple tempo- and meter-beat patterns from notation (SA)
15. recognize and clap/chant/play familiar duple and triple tempo- and meter-beat patterns within notation of familiar songs (CS)
16. recognize and clap/chant/play familiar duple and triple tempo- and meter-beat patterns within notation of unfamiliar songs (G) (At this point, overlap objectives by simultaneously beginning a content sequence at number 7 with unusual meter patterns that elongate underlying tempo and meter beats or subdivide meter beats)
17. improvise, compose, and perform combinations of familiar written duple and triple tempo- and meter-beat rhythm patterns (C/I)
18. understand the theoretical basis for metric function of duple and triple tempo- and meter-beat patterns (TU)

This list of objectives provides a sequence of content within a sequence for learning. This is an example of how analysis of content and instructional sequence facilitates diagnostic and prescriptive teaching. The reader is reminded that the process may not necessarily make teaching easier but should make for more effective teaching. Here is a summary outline of the rhythm content sequence embedded within the above list of objectives:

Sing a repertoire of rote songs in duple and triple meter feeling

Move with a consistent tempo-beat feeling to music

Move to consistent duple meter-beat feeling to music

Move to consistent triple meter-beat feeling to music

Recognize songs as duple or triple meter feeling

Develop a melodic rhythm pattern vocabulary of

    duple and triple meter patterns

        patterns that coincide with tempo and meter beats

        patterns that subdivide meter beats

        patterns that elongate across tempo beats

Utilize patterns in usual duple meter signatures (2, 4 as upper number)

Utilize patterns in usual triple meter signatures (3, 6, sometimes 9, 12 as upper number)

Utilize patterns in unusual meter signatures (5, 7, sometimes 9 as upper number)

The task of teaching rhythmic feeling must relate more to body movement than eye movement. Following the sequence of learning the sounds of rhythms, labeling with syllables and meter names, and then emphasizing the rhythm symbols as representing familiar sounds allows instrumentalists to develop their rhythmic potential effectively.

Review Questions

1. What is rhythmic feeling?
2. What is tempo-beat feeling?
3. What is meter-beat feeling?
4. What are melodic rhythm patterns?
5. Why should beginning instrumentalists develop a rhythm-pattern vocabulary?
6. What constitutes the Aural/Oral level for a sense of rhythmic feeling?
7. What are some activities for developing tempo-beat feeling?
8. What are some activities for developing meter-beat feeling?
9. Why should beginning instrumentalists work with songs in moderate tempos?
10. How are rhythm patterns taught with verbal association?
11. What are some criteria for choosing a set of rhythm syllables, and how should they be used within learning skills sequence?
12. Why is it useful to switch meters of familiar songs, and how is it accomplished?
13. When and how should beginning instrumentalists be introduced to rhythm notation?
14. How may writing rhythm patterns be incorporated in instruction?
15. What is the rationale for interpreting meter signatures?
16. Why are all duple patterns first notated with two-quarter meter signatures and triple patterns with six-eighth meter signatures?
17. What is the sequence for moving to meter signatures other than two-quarter and six-eighth?
18. What is the inconsistency often found in teaching rhythmic feeling in tunes notated with three-quarter meter signatures?
19. What is the relationship of meter signatures and note values to tempo of music?

20. What are some composite synthesis activities for learning rhythm patterns?
21. Considering the rhythm pattern 1-ne-ta, what would be an appropriate teaching technique at each level of Gordon's learning sequence for beginning instrumentalists?
22. How does teaching dotted notation through rhythm patterns differ from the traditional process?
23. How might inference learning of rhythm patterns be encouraged?
24. What are some of the considerations that often cause difficulties in interpreting rhythm notation with rhythmic feeling?
25. What are some criteria for choosing materials for teaching rhythmic feeling?
26. What is the sequence of rhythm content discussed in this chapter?

References

DEYARMAN, ROBERT. (1975). An experimental analysis of the development of rhythmic and tonal capabilities of kindergarten and first-grade children. *Experimental Research in the Psychology of Music: Studies in the Psychology of Music* 10, 1–23.
DITTEMORE, EDGAR E. (1970). An investigation of some musical capabilities of elementary school children. *Experimental Research in the Psychology of Music: Studies in the Psychology of Music* 6, 1–44.
GORDON, EDWIN E. (1971). *The psychology of music teaching.* Englewood Cliffs, NJ: Prentice-Hall, Inc.
———. (1993). *Learning sequences in music.* Chicago: GIA Publications, Inc.
HOVEY, NILO. (1976). *Efficient rehearsal procedures for school bands.* Elkhart, IN: The Selmer Co.
JAQUES-DALCROZE, ÉMILE. ([1921] 1967). *Rhythm, music and education,* trans. H. Rubenstein, rev. ed. of 1921 version. Redcourt, England: The Dalcroze Society, Inc.
MCHOSE, ALLEN, and RUTH N. TIBBS. (1945). *Sight-singing manual.* New York: Appleton-Century-Crofts.
MURSELL, JAMES L. and MABELLE GLENN. (1931). *The psychology of school music teaching.* New York: Silver Burdett Co.
PALMER, MARY. (1976). Relative effectiveness of two approaches to rhythm reading for fourth-grade students. *Journal of Research in Music Education* 24 (3), 110–118.

Teaching Performance Skills Through Pattern Vocabularies and Music

The two preceding chapters dealt with teaching of rhythm and tonal concepts in a carefully designed sequence of content and learning skills. The reality of the teaching-learning process with instrumental music is that a sense of tonality, a sense of rhythmic feeling, and technical skills must be taught concurrently on the instruments. Tonal and rhythmic concepts must be stressed with instrumental techniques in lessons and ensemble rehearsals. This chapter contains numerous examples and explanations of how instrumental skills may be acquired and musical results obtained. It is pointless to play an instrument if the results are not musical. Mursell and Glenn (1931, p. 302) comment that "our aim in instrumental music must be to teach the instrument through music and for the sake of music, and to use the instrument to refine, define, and make more ardent, the music-making impulse."

Types of Beginning Instrumental Instruction

Research has provided no conclusive evidence whether private instrumental instruction or group instruction produces greater musical achievement in school settings. Class instruction is the current norm in school settings, since it is difficult to justify private-lesson instruction in public schools when teacher time and efficiency per student are considered. Beginning class instruction may be found in groups of two to more than seventy. Class groups may comprise like instruments, instrument families, or randomly mixed instruments. Most instrumental teachers, including the author, prefer small group instruction for beginners with two to eight students per group. It is preferable for the groups to have like instruments initially in order to learn musical and instrumental skills efficiently. It is most helpful if students who receive weekly small-group instruction also participate weekly in a large ensemble of mixed instruments. The small-group lesson allows for more individualized attention to musical and technical needs of students, whereas the large ensemble affords opportunity to experience beginning band and orchestra music with emphasis on ensemble performance skills.

The key to effective class instruction is to meet the differing musical and technical needs of each individual within a group setting. This does not mean attending to one student at a time while the remainder sit and wait for their turn. Developing the musical potential of students requires involvement of the entire class in the learning process without necessarily having everyone do the same task at the same time. Class instruction techniques may also capitalize on peer-group learning and motivation. Group performance may be emphasized but must not exclude the development of musical independence and individual student needs.

Instrumental Techniques

Learning to perform on a musical instrument requires systematic accomplishment of skills for manipulating and operating the instrument. These performance techniques are also called executive skills and are prerequisite to producing musical sounds and expression with an instrument. The specific skills or techniques depend on the particular instrument to be studied. Typical instrumental techniques or executive skills include embouchure, bowing, hand positions, breath support, body posture, tonguing, tone quality, fingering patterns, intonation, and vibrato. Many of these techniques overlap and interact on an instrument; for example, tone quality is dependent on breath support, embouchure, and posture when playing a wind instrument.

Acquiring instrumental technique involves motor control and muscle training in addition to musical skills. Careful practice is necessary to learn how to express musical intent with an instrument. Frank R. Wilson (1981), a neurologist writing about motor skills and instrumental performance, states:

> Slow practice is the key to rapid technical progress. The cerebellum is a non-judgmental part of the brain; it assumes that any repetitive activity in the muscular system is being repeated because the conscious mind is trying to make it automatic. The cerebellum will be just as efficient an automatizer of incorrect sequences of timing as of those that are correct. When practicing takes place at a pace too fast for accurate playing, there is very little chance for the material to be mastered, and reliable, confident performance simply will not occur. On the other hand, it is probably true that practice for speed is seldom necessary. The cerebellum can supply all the speed wanted if patterning is correct during practice. (p. 14)

As was mentioned in Chapter 4, it is important to remember that when slowing down tempos for rehearsal purposes, do not change the location of where the tempo beat is felt. Fingerings for pitches may be practiced slowly without the rhythm or sound; rhythms may be practiced without the pitches; then place the section back into the correct rhythmic and tonal context.

Many method book authors and instrumental teachers emphasize extensive technique development with beginning students before considerable melodic material in familiar songs is attempted. Contrived exercises emphasize motor-skill development of fingering patterns and bowings. The primary objectives are mechanical rather than musical. This approach is consistent with many European music-conservatory practices, which began in the nineteenth century. Its continued advocacy in many private teaching studios, especially in universities, has influenced many school music instrumental teachers who, in turn, use the same techniques with beginning instrumentalists.

Sequences for introducing instrumental techniques and how the techniques should be taught have evolved over the years. Opinions often vary concerning such issues as the best beginning bow grip, the proportion of upper and lower lips in cup mouthpieces, when to introduce alternate fingerings, or how to teach vibrato. Practical experiences and a minimal research base underlie current practice. Most beginning-level instrument instruction books dwell on technical skills taught with music notation. Some materials introduce a few melodies in conjunction with technical exercises. A few instruction books do emphasize playing melodies without many added technical exercises.

Learning an instrument is much easier when tonal- and rhythm-pattern vocabularies are first developed in general music classes through singing and chanting. Instrumental teaching can then stress development of instrument skills as a means for expressing the familiar musical vocabulary. Unfortunately, most beginning instrumental students do not have adequate previous music vocabulary training and must be taught tonal and rhythmic content while learning an instrument; a less efficient, though possible, sequence of events.

Instrumental teachers need to assess prior musical achievement of beginning students so that appropriate musical instruction may be included with instrumental skills. Information to be gathered about each beginning instrumentalist should include use of singing voice, song repertoire, tonal and rhythmic strengths and weaknesses, and music reading facility. Data may be collected with group achievement tests (standardized and/or teacher-constructed), a standardized music aptitude test, and individual performance tests. Remember, knowing names of music symbols does not constitute functional music achievement. General music teachers may be able to provide much of the information needed; otherwise, the instrumental teacher should schedule time to complete the assessment of the beginner's prior music achievement.

Technical skill development can be logically coordinated with tonal and rhythm pattern vocabulary if the instrument is to be used to express musical ideas. Technical skill as an end in itself, however, merely becomes acrobatics. Students become too easily enamored with how fast their fingers can move or how high a pitch they can play rather than how musically they can perform. Motivation to perform musically is provided through integration of technical demands with musical content. Beginning instrumental instruction is most efficient in producing functional musicians when tonal and rhythmic-pattern content is related to melodic materials and is the basis for technical development. Instruction of advanced instrumentalists is facilitated by a foundation of musical and technical competence.

The most important instrumental skill to be developed is pleasing tone quality. Other instrumental skills and musical attempts are not

productive if a solid basis for tone production and quality is not established first. Acceptable tone quality is learned best through imitation
of live or recorded models of sound rather than verbal or written
descriptions. For example, Suzuki techniques for teaching stringed
instruments include extensive listening to recorded lesson materials
and also performing without notation. Both techniques are essential to
initial development of tone quality.

The first sounds produced on an instrument should not be considered as isolated pitches but rather as components of familiar tonal patterns consisting of two to five pitches. Careful attention to the skills
necessary to produce good tone quality is essential at all times, but the
eventual goal is to perform accurate tonal patterns that were previously learned with tonal syllables. These first tonal patterns should be
performed without notation. Emphasis is only directed to accurate
pitches with good tone quality in pattern configurations. Correct fingerings should be demonstrated by the teacher and may be verbally
labeled with the note names. *Extending the range and learning new fingerings is accomplished by moving the same familiar tonal patterns to new
pitch locations.* The decision about what fingerings to introduce and
when to introduce them is not necessarily dependent on a particular
method book sequence but rather is made by choosing a new key
and/or mode for a familiar pattern or tune. Choice of patterns depends
on tonal-pattern-content sequence as discussed in Chapter 3.

A First Lesson Example

A musical objective for the first lesson on a woodwind instrument
could be to teach the familiar patterns M R̲ D̲ and D R̄ M̄. (It is
assumed that students can sing the two patterns accurately with tonal
syllables.) The two patterns may be performed with left-hand fingerings only. Thumb and first finger (T-1) produce *mi*, and T-1-2 produce
re, and T-1-2-3 produce *do*. M R̲ D̲ is easily learned by adding one finger at a time, and D R̄ M̄ by simply removing one finger for each pitch.
Students should first hear the teacher perform the patterns and
observe the fingerings. A pattern should then be sung with tonal syllables and then sung again with syllables while practicing the fingerings. Performing the patterns with instruments may then begin.

Remember that notation and rhythm are not taught at his point. The assignment now is to use the two tonal patterns to play three familiar tunes: "Hot Cross Buns," "At Pierrot's Door" (first half), and "Mary Had a Little Lamb." If a student does not know one of the songs, the song is first learned by rote through singing the words.

Move the patterns and tunes to a new pitch level during the first lesson. It is essential to move them no later than the second lesson so that tonal syllables do not become primarily associated with specific fingerings. It is important to learn that the pitch produced with each fingering may be used for any tonal syllable. A suggested order for woodwinds would be to move next to right-hand fingers only while left-hand fingers remain down. The fingering pattern for right hand only M R̲ D̲ and D R̄ M̄ varies, depending on which woodwind instrument is used. The patterns may next be moved to a pitch level that requires movement of fingers on both hands; for example, F, G, and A on flute, saxophone, and oboe. Each time the patterns are moved, the teacher should first demonstrate the new fingerings, and students should sing with the syllables while doing the fingerings, perform the patterns with instruments, and then practice the three-note tunes without notation. Introduce whatever correct fingerings are necessary to perform the patterns and tunes. By the second lesson, the same process should begin for teaching D T̲ L̲ and L T̄ D̄ patterns for tonic minor function. The three tunes may be switched to minor mode using the new patterns. Again, move the patterns to different pitch levels as soon as possible. Range expansion and number of fingerings learned will proceed rapidly for most students.

This pattern sequence is directly adaptable to brasses, strings, mallet percussion, and keyboards. Three-valve brasses may begin in midrange; for example, trumpet: C, D, E, then move to D, E, F-sharp and E, F-sharp, G-sharp. Strings should play the patterns on each string. Keyboard instruments have complete flexibility of pitch location, including octaves, and students should be encouraged to utilize the entire keyboard.

The two tonal patterns are initially performed without rhythm-pattern interaction. Ordinarily, students will be able to perform the three-note tunes with correct rhythms because they are familiar with them through singing. Consistent tempo-beat and meter-beat feeling should be stressed while performing the songs. Watch for fingering coordination problems, which cause breakdowns in rhythmic flow. Return to singing the patterns and songs while doing the fingerings whenever necessary.

The advantages of these procedures are many. Musical sound and tone quality are always emphasized first. The student's goal is to produce familiar musical sounds. Learning new fingerings and technical development is facilitated with a minimal tonal-pattern vocabulary. Students have musical reasons to use the fingerings and to strive for good sounds. Fingering patterns and coordination are learned without pointless drill activities. Technique becomes an outgrowth of musical practice. A sense of tonality is reinforced through the two tonal patterns in major and two more in minor. Through use of the familiar tunes and tonal patterns, students can remember how they should sound during practices that are not supervised by the instructor.

It is important to remember that the previous example of content and technique is accomplished without notation. Notation of the patterns and the three-note tunes should be introduced at appropriate pitch levels *after* students demonstrate their ability to perform the tunes. Names of notes are initially associated with fingerings, so pitch levels may be designated (e.g., "Play with *do* as G"). After learning to perform a tune at a new pitch level, students might be shown the new notation for D R̄ M̄ and M R̲ D̲ and then asked to write out the pitches for the tune (rhythm may or may not be notated, depending on the student's rhythm achievement level).

It may be particularly important if students are not seen more than once or twice a week for instruction that they take along something in written form to aid their practice. Figure 5.1, a suggested worksheet example to send with students after their first lesson, follows. Adjust content as needed.

Rhythm Patterns and Instrument Skills

Familiar rhythm patterns may be used for articulation practice on all instruments. Tonguing or bowing, for instance, can be developed while performing rhythm patterns on assigned pitches with set tempos. Familiar rhythm patterns should be used without notation. Teachers should always refer to rhythm patterns with correct syllables rather

Do	Re	Mi		Mi	Re	Do
C	D	E				
D	E	F♯				
B♭	C	D				
F	G	A				

Write in the letter names for the *mi-re-do* pattern.

Practice singing the *do-re-mi* and *mi-re-do* patterns.

Practice singing the patterns while doing the fingerings you know for each letter name before blowing into your instrument.

Practice playing the patterns. Always listen for good tone quality.

Sing and play "Hot Cross Buns" and "Mary Had a Little Lamb."

Some things to remember:

Breathe deeply when playing your instrument.

Always check posture and hand positions before playing.

Practice before a mirror to check embouchure and hand positions while playing.

PRACTICE EVERY DAY

Figure 5.1   TRUMPET AND CLARINET WORKSHEET

than note values. Verbal instructions, for example, should be "Play 1 ne ta 2 ne on G" rather than "Play an eighth note, two sixteenth notes, and two eighths on G." By giving instructions that refer to rhythmic feeling instead of asking for a particular written-note value to be performed on a given pitch, students relate to their rhythm pattern vocabulary. Consistent tempo beat and meter beat feeling should be stressed at all times when students chant or perform rhythm patterns.

A series of wind instrument articulation exercises on a given pitch with four tempo beats per line in a moderate speed might proceed with the teacher instructing the student as follows:

1. Tongue on each tempo beat
2. Tongue on   1   ne   2   ne

3. Tongue on	1 ta	ne ta	2 ta	ne ta			
4. Tongue on	1	ne ta	2	ne ta			
5. Tongue on	1 ta	ne	2 ta	ne			
6. Tongue on	1	na	ni	2	na	ni	
7. Tongue on	1 ta	na	ta ni	ta 2 ta	na	ta ni	ta
8. Tongue on	1	na	ta ni	ta 2	na	ta ni	ta
9. Tongue on	1 ta	na	ta ni	2 ta	na	ta ni	

The relationship to the underlying rhythmic feeling is established for each of these suggested exercises through verbal reference to the syllables used for the desired pattern and not to note-value names. Begin practicing by setting a moderate speed for the tempo beats. If using a metronome, set the beats per minute for the tempo-beat speed. Patterns should be chanted with syllables before being performed on the instrument. The speed for each exercise may be gradually increased as students gain proficiency, but the underlying rhythmic feeling remains constant. Tonal interaction is minimized by using only one pitch for the rhythm and articulation practice. The objective for students is to perform a familiar rhythm pattern accurately with precise articulation.

Rhythmic variations of familiar melodies may be performed by changing the melodic rhythm patterns but not the pitches. A rhythmic variation of a melody will not follow the rhythm of the words but will retain the pitch relationships. Articulation and new rhythm patterns may be practiced without the connotations of drill. Students should be encouraged to choose patterns to devise their own rhythm variations of familiar tunes. The more variety of rhythm patterns in the melody, the more possibilities of articulation variations. The following example uses the first line of "Twinkle, Twinkle, Little Star" to show how the entire melodic rhythm might be changed. The tonal syllables change with each tempo beat in this example and are included under the words. The first line of rhythm syllables under the text fits the original version, and the remaining lines are some of the possible melodic rhythm-pattern variations:

Twin-kle,		twin-kle, lit-		tle	star,
Do		So	La		So
1	ne	2	ne 1	ne	2

Duple variations

```
1  ta  ne  ta  2  ta  ne  ta  1  ta  ne  ta  2  ta  ne  ta
1  ta      ta  2  ta      ta  1  ta      ta  2  ta      ta
1  ta          2  ta          1  ta          2  ta
1      ta  2          ta  1              ta  2              ta
```

Triple variations

```
1      ni  2      ni  1      ni  2      ni
1  na      2  na      1  na      2  na
```

The melodic rhythm pattern for each tempo beat in the example is performed without altering the tonal outline of the original melody. The same melodic rhythm pattern variations may be repeated throughout the tune, or each phrase could use a different pattern. Tonguing and slurring or bowing patterns may be superimposed on the rhythm patterns. Students should be encouraged to perform and write down their own rhythmic variations of familiar melodies.

Tonal Patterns and Instrument Skills

One of the most useful applications of tonal patterns with instrumental technique is to select excerpts that are awkward or difficult to finger with facility and treat them as tonal patterns within a musical context. Specific patterns will vary depending on the instrument and the student, but in any case, students should be asked to audiate and sing the pattern first so they demonstrate awareness of the desired pitches. The next step might be to practice the fingerings while singing the pattern and then perform the pattern. The melodic rhythm may be ignored until smooth fingering technique with the pitches is apparent. Students perform the pattern in rhythm within the musical phrase.

Other possibilities include introducing lip slurs as tonal patterns for brass instrument performers to develop lip flexibility. Intonation of octave intervals and arpeggios may be taught through tonal patterns for all instruments. Fingering patterns on stringed instruments and keyboards may be introduced as tonal patterns.

Scales

Scale exercises are included in most instrumental books and are most often taught as fingering or theory exercises rather than tonal or rhythmic studies. Scales are not tonal patterns as defined in Chapter 3, but they may be used to develop a sense of tonality. Scales may be sung with tonal syllables before performing with an instrument, and they may be divided into segments that are learned as tonal patterns. The ascending major scale would be constructed of D R̄ M̄F and S L̄ T̄ D̄ or D R̄ M̄F S̄ and L T̄ D̄ or D R̄ M̄ and F S̄ L̄ T̄ D̄. The ascending harmonic minor scale could be constructed of L T̄ D̄R̄ and M F̄ Si L or L T̄ D̄R̄ M̄ and F S̄i L̄ or L T̄ D̄ and R M̄F S̄i L̄. The patterns may be learned separately and then connected to build scales in all keys. The student objective is to perform familiar tonal patterns in scale configurations while acquiring acceptable fingering technique. These same tonal patterns derived from scales become a part of melodic pattern vocabulary when they appear in melodies.

Most instrumental materials emphasize major scales and only a few minor scales. As explained in Chapter 3, initial tonal content should include about half major and half minor songs, so scale study material should parallel these proportions. Scales should be practiced in all keys for finger facility and range extension. When students can perform songs in modes other than major and minor, corresponding scale studies should eventually be included in other modes. Again, tonal patterns may be used to learn the scales in the new modes. For example, the ascending mixolydian scale could be constructed from S L̄ T̄ D̄and R M̄ F̄ S̄ or S L̄ T̄ D̄R and M F̄ S̄ or S L̄ T̄ and D R̄ M̄ F̄ S̄. The dorian scale could be constructed from R M̄ F̄ S̄ and L T̄ D̄R or R M̄F S̄ L̄ and T D̄R̄ or R M̄ F̄ and S L̄ T̄ D̄R̄. It should become apparent that the same tonal patterns and fingering patterns occur in different combinations to construct various scales. Only the harmonic function of the tonal patterns changes with new scale locations. Students should be able to perform and notate the scales in all modes and in all keys after careful, consistent study. Attention should be drawn to tonal patterns from scales and the related fingering patterns when they occur in melodies. Rhythm patterns and various articulation patterns may also be combined with scale studies. Each scale degree may be assigned a

rhythm pattern or series of patterns to be performed with a given articulation pattern. The objective for the student is now threefold—to
perform rhythm patterns, tonal patterns, and articulation patterns
accurately. For example, assign the ascending and descending C-major
scale, each pitch to be performed on 1 ne ta 2 ta ne, and with staccato
articulation on all notes.

Diatonic ascending and descending scales may be altered with
tonal-pattern variations for further study material. Scales in thirds are
a common example. Rather than concentrate only on the new fingering patterns, the tonal patterns should be the primary learning goal.
An ascending major scale in thirds could be considered as a series of
two-tone patterns: D $\bar{\text{M}}$, R $\bar{\text{F}}$, M $\bar{\text{S}}$, F $\bar{\text{L}}$, S $\bar{\text{T}}$, L $\bar{\text{D}}$, plus T $\bar{\text{R}}$ $\underline{\text{D}}$. A predetermined rhythm pattern and articulation could also be assigned to
each pitch, to add complexity. Arpeggio studies such as those
described in Chapter 3 in Table 3.1 and Figure 3.3 are also useful fingering exercises and may be given added difficulty with assigned
rhythms and articulations in a variety of keys and modes.

Changing Keys, Modes, and Meters

Transposition occurs whenever a melody is moved to a new pitch level
with a corresponding key signature change. Transposition is usually
considered an advanced technique and then taught as an intervallic
and theoretical exercise with notation. The result is that most instrumentalists are not accomplished in transposition. Transposition of
melodies is a useful technique for acquiring instrumental technique
and expanding ranges. It need not be difficult or advanced if intervals,
notation, and theory are initially avoided. Transposition begins in the
first lessons without notation by shifting initial tonal patterns and
melodies to different starting pitches on the instrument. This allows
new fingerings to be learned and range to extend without need for
additional material. All students should regularly be expected to move
familiar tunes and patterns to different pitch locations without notation. Later, as facility for reading and writing notation develops, students should be expected to write patterns and melodies at various
pitch levels. Transposition skills are established by continued practice
as new materials are introduced. Eventually, even complex patterns
may be performed with minimal difficulty at various pitch levels.

The techniques for changing modes and meters were described in Chapters 3 and 4. Musical and technical skills are developed by these techniques. Difficulty and complexity of assignments can be increased by combining key, mode, and meter changes with songs. More advanced students may be challenged while less complex tasks are assigned to less advanced students. For example, an advanced student might be asked to play "Yankee Doodle," first learned in F major and duple, in the relative key and mode of d minor and in triple meter. A less advanced student might be asked to play the tune in F major and in triple.

Additional Musical Content

Tonal and rhythmic content can be the basis for developing instrumental technique, and is also the foundation for additional musical considerations. Specifically, musical style, phrasing, tempos, dynamics, harmony, and form may be taught through tonal and rhythm pattern vocabularies and familiar melodies.

Style training begins with articulation of tonal and rhythm patterns. Staccato, marcato, and legato performance of pitches in patterns and songs should begin within the first few lessons. Familiar songs should be practiced with each articulation style. Phrasing is best introduced through singing the words of songs and then performing with instruments to imitate the sung phrases. It is preferable if melodies for beginning instrumentalists include the words, so that singing of phrases can be easily practiced. The concept of ending phrases where a line of text ends and a breath is normally taken should be taught to all instrumentalists, regardless of instrument. The interactions of tempo changes with style and phrasing may be studied through pattern vocabulary and melodic material. Providing listening examples as aural models of performance styles such as jazz, Mozart, Joplin, and marches allows for appropriate application of stylistic techniques in musical contexts.

Beginning instrumentalists should learn to perform their repertoire of patterns and songs with contrasting dynamics. Although most beginning materials ignore dynamic markings, the concepts of playing soft, medium loud, and loud need to be stressed as soon as acceptable tone quality is produced. More gradations of dynamics, including controlled crescendo and decrescendo, may be introduced as instrumental skills become more secure. Expressive performance at all levels must include control of dynamics.

Clarinetist preparing a solo with teacher accompanying

The arpeggio worksheet included in Chapter 3 as Figure 3.3 is an example of material for performing harmony lines. Rounds, simple duets, partner songs, trios, quartets, and quintets are also helpful in developing the awareness of harmonic progressions and lines. Many students are capable of improvising harmony lines to familiar melodies and should be expected to do so without notation. After facility with writing notation has begun, harmony lines may become written assignments. Class lesson groups may compose and perform their own small-ensemble arrangements.

Tonal and rhythmic content may also serve as the basis for learning about musical forms. Patterns may be combined and grouped to teach concepts of repetition, contrasting sections, variations, and thematic development. Composition assignments may include common forms such as rondo, ABA, AABA, and theme and variations. Students may devise variations of melodies by changing tonal and rhythm patterns, articulations, modes, meters, keys, dynamics, and so on. Worksheets may be constructed that incorporate many possible tonal, rhythm, and technique tasks. Figure 5.2 gives an example of a worksheet with suggested assignments. Provide students with such a worksheet after they are familiar through singing and playing the songs "Lightly Row," "Go

_____1. Lightly row, lightly row, o'er the glassy waves we go

_____2. Twinkle, twinkle, little star

_____3. Go tell Aunt Rhody her old gray goose is dead

_____4. Merrily, merrily, merrily, merrily, life is but a dream

_____5. Let the wind and waters be mingled with our melody

_____6. Up above the world so high

_____7. He stuck a feather in his cap and called it macaroni

_____8. Go tell Aunt Rhody, go tell her right away

_____9. Row, row, row your boat gently down the stream

_____10. Yankee Doodle went to town a-riding on a pony

Figure 5.2   PHRASE WORKSHEET

Tell Aunt Rhody," "Yankee Doodle," "Row, Row, Row Your Boat," and "Twinkle, Twinkle, Little Star."

Many possibilities exist for activities with the worksheet for checking tonal and rhythmic learning. For each of the ten items, some examples organized as tonal, rhythm, and performance tasks are:

TONAL ACTIVITIES
- Students indicate the mode by placing M or *m* in the blank
- Teacher performs pitches without rhythm and students match to the item number
- Students mark the location of the resting tone pitch for the song with an X under the corresponding word or syllable
- Students write appropriate tonal syllables under the words
- Given staff paper, students notate correct pitches for each line

RHYTHM ACTIVITIES
- Students mark the location of the tempo beats with an X
- Students indicate the meter by placing a D or T in the blank
- Teacher performs melodic rhythm without pitches for the lines and students match to the item number

- Students place *p c* or *p c c* under appropriate words or syllables to indicate meter-beat locations
- Students write the appropriate rhythm syllables under the words and syllables
- Students write appropriate rhythm notation under words and syllables

PERFORMANCE ACTIVITIES
- Students accurately sing each line
- Students clap the melodic rhythm of each line
- Students accurately perform each line without notation on their instrument
- Students perform each line in two or more keys and indicate the number of keys
- Students perform each line in two octave levels

Making Choices

Instrumental technique and musical skills can progress with interest and motivation when students have the opportunity to make choices about using their musical capabilities. Opportunities for musical growth occur by involving learners in decisions about how many different ways familiar songs may be performed. Some possible choices are displayed in the following list:

Key: C-flat, D-flat, A-flat, E-flat, B-flat, F, C, D, A, E, B, F-sharp, C-sharp

Mode: major, minor, dorian, mixolydian, phrygian, lydian

Meter: duple, triple, unusual

Tempo: slow, moderate, fast

Articulation: legato, marcato, staccato

Dynamics: Soft, medium soft, medium loud, loud

Any given melody could be practiced and performed in many combinations of choices taken from the six categories. "Yankee Doodle" is usually first learned in F major, duple, moderate, marcato, and medium loud. The song may be used to learn many musical and technical skills by changing one category at a time. Eventually, all categories may change from the original version—D minor, triple, fast, staccato, and soft—and the song takes on a new character. After learning a familiar song, students may use the above list to determine what new version to practice. It should not be necessary to notate new versions before performance, but written assignments may be generated with the list. The list should be built gradually as students acquire facility in each category. Songs should be taken through as many combinations of categories as are practical and of interest to students. The objective for the students is to function with their musical and technical skills through musical manipulation of familiar songs.

Improvisation

One of the basic indicators of technical facility and proficiency with an instrument is the ability to improvise. Performing musical ideas that are first audiated and then expressed through an instrument is a higher-order process and demands a melding of knowledge and skill. In many cultures, the primary music-making activity is improvisation of rhythms and melodies. In western European musical tradition, improvisation was an expected and highly valued skill for most instrumentalists during the Baroque period (1600–1750). Since that era, however, art music has devalued improvisation skills, even though many famous musicians such as Mozart and Beethoven were highly regarded as improvisors. Today in this country, improvisation skills are expected of instrumentalists in idioms such as folk, country, rock, and jazz. Jazz ensembles in schools provide limited opportunities for students to develop and use improvisation skills. Because improvisation is not usually taught or encouraged at beginning levels of instruction, most students are introduced to the skills through music notation and theory after they reach high school. Notation reading rather than audiation skills is emphasized, and proficiency levels of improvisation skills suffer. The majority of instrumentalists trained in our schools learn to perform ensemble and solo literature through practice and repetition but fail to function with their instrument as a means to improvise and express musical ideas.

We know from experience and research that school instrumentalists can profit from early and continued training and expectations in improvisation. Technical skills and musical skills are enhanced with this training. Building vocabularies of tonal and rhythm patterns with audiation and technical skills is the basis for improvisation facility. As noted in Chapter 1, the recent National Standards for Arts Education includes improvisation as the third standard for music; and as mentioned in Chapter 2, Gordon includes improvisation as part of the inference-learning section of his learning-skills sequence. Studies by Mainwaring (1941), Luce (1965), and Priest (1989) emphasize the importance of "thinking in sound" and "playing by ear." Webster (1990, 1994) advocates audiation training and improvisation activities as basic to school music instruction. He also recommends use of music software by children as a means to develop critical and creative musical thinking. McPherson (1993) found that a high school instrumentalist's ability to improvise is not predictable from length of study but is mainly influenced by early enriching activities, especially playing by ear. He also found that the strongest predictor of sight-reading skills for high school students was the ability to play by ear. In a study with fifth-grade instrumental students, Azzara (1993) reports that those with improvisation instruction, which included playing by ear, singing, and verbal association with tonal and rhythm patterns, scored significantly higher on performance achievement tests than those taught without improvisation emphasis.

Improvisation skills should be encouraged and developed as students acquire pattern vocabularies and technical skills. This is essential for functioning as an instrumental musician, in addition to reading music notation proficiently. Some published materials that include recordings designed for training improvisation skills are listed at the end of this chapter.

Composing Music

Instrumental music in today's schools is primarily geared to performance of published music materials. Music composition activities, if encouraged or assigned at all, are usually reserved for music theory classes or "gifted" students and are not generally considered to be a necessary part of instrumental instruction. Beginning in the mid-1960s, the Manhattanville Music Curriculum Program (MMCP) included an instrumental component where students were expected to compose their own music instead of using published materials (Mark, 1996, p. 138). With few exceptions, MMCP ideas have not taken hold in school instrumental music curricula. Nevertheless, educators and researchers continue to call for composition activities as an important part of music learning (Gardner, 1993; Gordon, 1993). The National Standards for Arts Education includes composing as the fourth content standard for music.

Research by Kratus (1994a) is helping to reveal the process of music composition by children. He finds that there is a definite link between audiation and certain aspects of music creativity, and he theorizes that audiation is an indicator of a sense of tonality and meter. This, in turn, results in a framework for composition to occur. Kratus (1994b) identifies three main composition processes as exploration, development, and repetition, and he recommends that music educators value and include these processes in their instruction. By helping students learn how to write music compositions, their music creativity may be expressed with facility similar to speaking and writing language.

Can composition training improve instrumental performance? The process of audiation is prerequisite and corequisite for composing music. If audiation skills are developed through composition activity, instrumental skills can only be enhanced. Instrumental students should be trained in the composition process through using their tonal and rhythm pattern vocabularies.

Sight-reading

The ability to perform music at sight is a highly desired skill for instrumentalists. As with improvisation, a combination of proficient technique and musical skills is required. True sight-reading entails performing from notation a selection that is unfamiliar aurally or visually. The process is basically a matter of transfer from the known to the unknown, bringing to bear the familiar musical vocabulary and technical skills on the notation of an unfamiliar composition. The transfer process can be facilitated and practiced. As described in Chapter 2, Gordon refers to this as generalization in his learning sequence.

In the previous section on improvisation, it is stated that McPherson found the strongest predictor of high school students' sight-reading ability is their facility to play by ear. He also found the majority of sight-reading errors by these students to be rhythm related. His research supports the contention that sight-reading can be taught, and he proposes that the process involves

(a) the ability to seek information relevant to an accurate interpretation prior to the commencement of the musical performance. This involves observing the key and time signature of the work together with an ability to scan the music briefly in order to maximize comprehension and to identify possible obstacles;
(b) a brief period of mental rehearsal of the major difficulties before commencing to play;
(c) the directing and maintaining of attention throughout the performance in order to anticipate problems and to observe musical indications (such as expression markings and articulation) indicated above and below the musical line; and
(d) self-monitoring and evaluation of the response in order to correct the performance when errors occur. This includes being able to match the information obtained visually from the notation with aural feedback of the sound being produced to monitor and evaluate success. (McPherson, 1994, p. 229)

Sight-reading skills should be developed through careful building of tonal and rhythm pattern vocabularies, audiation skills, playing by ear, technical skills, and regular practice with unfamiliar notation. Applying strategies such as those recommended by McPherson is also an important part of the process. These strategies should begin when students are expected to perform from notation most of the time and should not be delayed until intermediate or advanced levels of instruction.

Diagnosis and Prescription

Instrumentalists must attend to many variables in order to function and perform musically. Effective teachers must be able to diagnose and correct instrumental performance problems when they occur. The teacher must first discern that a problem exists, then determine specifically what the problem is, and lastly decide what to do and how to make corrections. Diagnosis is facilitated by organizing possible problems into two categories—instrumental technique and musical content. Each category may be subdivided into various components. The appropriate level of learning sequence must be determined as it interacts with musical content. Materials and teaching techniques are then chosen that are used to help solve the performance problem. Efficiency of teaching/learning and chances for student success improve greatly when teachers apply an organizational structure to problem solving rather than random, nonsystematic techniques. Diagnostic and prescriptive teaching should gain effectiveness through continued teaching experience.

In the following figure, the Diagnosis section contains two columns. The column on the left displays categories for labeling most common instrumental performance errors in musical content and instrument technique. The middle column lists the learning sequence for use with tonal and rhythm patterns when diagnosing problems. The Prescription column would be filled in by the teacher with appropriate materials, teaching techniques, and activities to meet the diagnosed need of individual students or classes.

The musical content and instrumental techniques listed above are not intended to be all-inclusive but are rather meant to provide broad classifications that cover most instrumental performance errors. Diagnosis includes determination of the problem, and in the case of rhythm or tonal errors, what level of learning sequence is involved. In order to think diagnostically, rhythm and tonal content sequence within the learning sequence must be followed. Logical ordering of prerequisites is essential for effective prescriptive content and techniques. Instrument techniques and musical content continuously interact. Instrument techniques are developed as a result of the musical content sequence, and musical content may be chosen to teach specific instrument techniques.

Learning Sequence and Diagnosis/Prescription

Using the Gordon skills learning sequence can be an efficient means to diagnose tonal and rhythmic pattern learning problems and to prescribe the next appropriate task. The learning-skills level for any given tonal or rhythmic pattern is readily assessed. Knowledge of the sequence then permits effective choice of each succeeding step for the

DIAGNOSIS	PRESCRIPTION	
(problem is due to)	(where in learning sequence)	(appropriate materials and teaching technique)
Musical Content	Aural/Oral	
Tonal or Rhythmic	Verbal Association	
Key	Partial Synthesis	
Mode	Symbolic Association	
Meter	Composite Synthesis	
Tempo	Generalization	
Arcticulation, Style	Creativity/Improvisation	
Dynamics	Theoretical Understanding	
Instrumental Technique		
Tone quality		
Embouchure		
Bowing		
Posture		
Holding position		
Breath support		
Tonguing		
Finger technique		
Intonation		
Tuning		

Figure 5.3   GUIDELINES FOR SOLVING
PERFORMANCE PROBLEMS

student. The following examples list a teaching activity at each learning sequence level for a given pattern to be taught:

Rhythm Pattern

- Aural/Oral—teacher claps pattern, student echo-claps
- Verbal Association—teacher chants pattern, student echo-chants
- Partial Synthesis—student aurally recognizes pattern in a familiar song
- Symbolic Association—student sees pattern on a flash card and chants syllables

- Composite Synthesis—student visually recognizes pattern in a familiar song
- Generalization—student aurally or visually recognizes pattern in an unfamiliar song
- Creativity/Improvisation—student includes the pattern in a rhythm improvisation or composition
- Theoretical Understanding—student learns the proportionality of note values within the pattern

Tonal Pattern

- Aural/Oral—teacher sings pattern on *lu*, student echo-sings/plays the pattern
- Verbal Association—teacher sings pattern with syllables, student echo-sings/plays
- Partial Synthesis—student aurally recognizes pattern in a familiar song
- Symbolic Association—student sees pattern on a flash card and sings and/or plays it
- Composite Synthesis—student visually recognizes pattern in a familiar song
- Generalization—student aurally or visually recognizes pattern in an unfamiliar song
- Creativity/Improvisation—student utilizes the pattern in a composition
- Theoretical Understanding—student learns the interval names within the pattern

If a student is unable to perform a pattern at any given sequence level, the teacher should drop back one step before moving forward again. Appropriate teaching techniques should be chosen for each level. Decisions always include whether the material or patterns are familiar or unfamiliar and if notation is or is not included in the task. The pacing and timing of moving from level to level will vary with individual students. It should not be expected or demanded that all students in a group do the same activity level at the same time. For example, in a class lesson, some students could be asked to echo-sing a pattern with syllables while others echo-play the pattern, or an advanced student might write patterns on the chalkboard for others to perform. Students should perform patterns as soon as they can consistently demonstrate correct verbal associations with syllables. Patterns should be performed at different pitch levels.

An example of procedures that incorporate learning sequence skills for a student who has trouble performing a written passage of music is as follows:

1. Without notation, the student echoes the teacher by singing the correct pitches using the words of the song or a neutral syllable such as "loo" (A/O) and then uses moveable *do* syllables without the rhythm (VA)
2. Student sings the passage from notation without the rhythm while doing the fingerings (SA)
3. Student plays the passage from notation without rhythm and emphasizes correct intonation, tone production, and fingerings (SA) (The teacher may relate the passage to appropriate chord arpeggios or provide chordal accompaniment)
4. Student chants rhythm syllables of the passage with consistent tempo-beat feeling (SA); if needed, revert to echo-chanting the patterns without notation before proceeding (VA)
5. Student performs fingerings in correct rhythm without sound (SA)
6. Student performs the passage with correct tone production, intonation, fingerings, articulations, and rhythm (CS)

Sequencing Technical Skills

Technical skills refer to the tasks necessary to manipulate an instrument and produce musical results. Various teachers may advocate differing techniques and sequences of steps to achieve desired results. When and how to introduce vibrato is a common example. Students may also differ in how they respond to various techniques.

Two important tenets when teaching instrument techniques are 1) break all tasks of instrument manipulation into a sequence of small steps, and 2) model each task whenever possible rather than verbalizing. Here is an example of the steps for teaching how to form a clarinet embouchure. Each step is to be modeled by the teacher, with added description only if the student has a problem imitating the model.

Grip the barrel joint with assembled mouthpiece, wetted reed, and ligature in the right hand with the reed turned toward your body

With mouth open, space upper and lower teeth about three-eighths inch apart (approximately the width of a pencil)

Point the chin downward, flattening against the teeth and lower jaw

Roll about half of the red of the lower lip over the lower teeth

Insert the mouthpiece and place the upper teeth on the mouthpiece about one-quarter to three-eighths inch from tip; the chin must remain flat, firm, and stretched downward

Rest the reed on the lower lip at the point where the reed touches the lay of the mouthpiece; the angle of the mouthpiece and barrel should now be about 45 degrees to the perpendicular face

Pull in the corners of the mouth firmly without biting or pinching on the reed

Blow a steady stream of air into the mouthpiece

Produce a concert pitch of approximately F-sharp, which indicates correct setting, firmness, and air support

With repetition and careful practice, these steps become automatic. As with tonal and rhythm vocabulary building, it is critical that correct habits be formed from the beginning. Obviously, embouchure formation is only a part of learning to produce musical sounds on a clarinet. Other sequences are necessary for instrument assembly, reed placement, hand positions, instrument holding, tonguing, and posture. Modeling each small step is much more efficient than describing it verbally. Teaching other instruments requires similar attention to detail. It is often helpful for students to use a mirror to see themselves while performing with correct technique. Accurate drawings or photographs of embouchure, posture, hand positions, and so forth are also useful references for students during unsupervised practice.

One of the reasons beginning instrumentalists gradually improve their technical skills on unfamiliar exercises or melodies is that teachers repeat the exercise or melody enough times that audiation begins to occur for the students. Adequate Aural/Oral experience is finally achieved. When students already "know" the melody, they are able to perform it with far fewer initial repetitions and technical difficulty. Often, what may appear to be a technique problem is in reality an audiation deficiency.

Class Lesson Example

This approximately forty-minute lesson is designed for a class of first-year clarinetists. It is intended as an example for the reader to follow the combining of tonal and rhythmic content with instrumental techniques. Prior to this lesson, the class has learned to read some familiar songs. No new rhythm patterns are presented in this lesson; however, some of the tonal patterns have not occurred previously for the class in this key. Teaching objectives of the lesson are

1. To review and/or learn the tonal patterns as listed in D major
2. To review the rhythm patterns as listed
3. To develop facility to finger A by rolling the left hand first finger
4. To change a familiar duple meter song to triple feeling
5. To change a familiar major song to minor mode

MATERIAL: SONG   *LIGHTLY ROW*
WORKSHEET NUMBER 1   (SEE FIGURE 5.4)

LESSON CHRONOLOGY:

• assemble instruments, check for workable reeds
• warm up with D R̄ M̄ F̄ S̄, D M̄ S̄, S M̲, F R̲ (echo-sing, check A fingering facility)
• sing through the song ("Is it a D M̄ S̄ or L D̄ M̄ song?" "Is it duple or triple feeling?")
• sing through the song while doing the fingerings, make corrections as needed
• perform song with instrument (check A fingering facility)
• sing song again while doing fingerings if necessary
• practice tonal patterns again if A fingering needs work
• find tonal patterns in the notation
• "Can anyone name other familiar songs that contain any of these tonal patterns?"
• sing song in minor (teacher gives i–V7–i introduction and chordal accompaniment)
• sing/play L T̄ D̄ R̄ M̄, L D̄ M̄, M D̲, R T̲ in D minor
• perform song in D minor ("What fingerings changed from the major version?")
• establish p-c-c feeling and sing/play in triple major
• sing in triple minor while doing fingerings
• perform on instrument in triple minor
• assignment: Next week perform "Lightly Row" and the tonal patterns in

Figure 5.4 MODEL FOR A SONG WORKSHEET

two new keys of your choice in duple and triple feeling. Practice one of the new versions with staccato articulation and the other with legato articulation. Write out the new versions in each key. Perform any other song or excerpt that uses some of the same tonal patterns.

The lesson example centers around musical content while developing fingering facility. Learning sequence is followed by moving from Aural/Oral activities through Synthesis and Generalization. Opportunities exist for class members to be doing different tasks simultaneously, such as singing, fingering, playing, and recognizing patterns. Rhythm problems are avoided by presenting only familiar patterns.

The second lesson example includes the song in Figure 5.5. This lesson is for beginning trumpet students who have a thorough understanding of duple and triple meter feeling and who regularly work with notation for duple and triple meter songs. No new tonal patterns are presented here, but this is the first song they have encountered in unusual meter feeling. No technique problems are anticipated for this class. This song sheet and activities may take only a portion of an entire lesson time. The teaching objectives are

1. To review the tonal patterns as listed in G major
2. To learn the rhythm patterns as listed
3. To change the song to triple meter feeling and perform it
4. To perform the song in a new key (use F major)

MATERIAL: SONG   *HOTDOG*
WORKSHEET NUMBER 2   (SEE FIGURE 5.5)

LESSON CHRONOLOGY:

- assemble instruments, check hand positions
- warm up with any of the listed tonal patterns
- teacher sings and plays the song
- teacher sings or plays the song while students sway from side to side on tempo-beat feeling and repeat p-c-c-p-c
- teacher sings song while students sing and do fingerings
- echo-chant the rhythm patterns as listed
- find rhythm patterns in the song notation
- students perform the song as written
- extract any problem tonal or rhythm patterns and review
- move *do* to F and practice tonal patterns
- perform the song in F major and unusual meter
- teacher and students do p-c-c-p-c-c feeling and sing the song with triple meter feeling
- students perform the song in triple meter feeling

Homework assignments include writing a harmony line with pitches on tempo beats only and writing out the song and performing it in other keys.

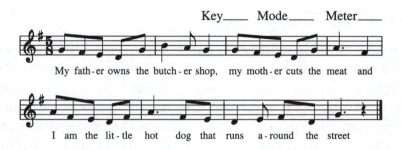

Key_____ Mode_____ Meter_____

My fath-er owns the butch-er shop, my moth-er cuts the meat and

I am the lit-tle hot dog that runs a-round the street

Rhythm Patterns:

du ba bi   du be   du   bi du   du   du

Tonal Patterns:

D T̲ L, S D̄, M R̲D, R T̄, R T̲ L, S T̄, S L̄ T̄

Assignments:

Perform in triple meter feeling

Perform in duple meter feeling

Write a harmony line with pitches on tempo beats only

Write out and perform in the keys of _____

_____

_____

Figure 5.5   UNUSUAL METER SONG WORKSHEET (FROM A
NICHOL'S WORTH, BK 1. TOMETIC ASSOCIATES, LTD., 1975.
REPRINTED BY PERMISSION OF DOUG NICHOL.)

Whenever students are expected to practice unsupervised at home, it is essential that lesson activities prepare for effective practice. Success in home practice is encouraged by assigning a familiar song but adding new technical and musical demands. It is wise to determine the learning sequence level asked of students in weekly assignments and make certain that prerequisites are accomplished. Musical preparations for the succeeding lesson should take place during instrumental lessons, so that home practice during intervening days may focus on perfecting instrumental technique problems within a musical context.

Rehearsal Warm-ups

Rehearsals of small and large ensembles are an ideal setting to incorporate musical and technical training. Technical skills may be developed through musical activities and materials. Effective rehearsing is a process of diagnosing performance problems and prescribing solutions. The first ten minutes or so of rehearsals are an opportunity to review pattern vocabularies, teach new patterns, and incorporate technique training.

The first few minutes of ensemble rehearsals and class lessons should be devoted to warm-up activities. With regard to wind instruments, Hovey (1976) states that the purposes of ensemble warm-up procedures are "(1) to bring the instrument to the temperature (and hence the pitch level) of normal playing, (2) to prepare the players' embouchures, and also correct reed placement and response, (3) to provide ear-training and encourage careful listening, (4) to develop good ensemble playing habits, and (5) to establish a mental set conducive to a successful rehearsal" (p. 13). Points 3–5 also apply to percussion, keyboard, and stringed instruments.

High school clarinet choir in rehearsal

The primary objective of a warm-up period should be to stress musical skills and instrumental techniques. Too often, warm-up time becomes only an attempt to blow warm air through horns, scratch with a bow, or pound with mallets and sticks while carelessly playing up and down a scale. Content for warm-up activities should center around tonal and rhythmic pattern vocabularies. The six categories of Key, Mode, Meter, Tempo, Articulation, and Dynamics provide a variety of musical considerations to be included in warm-ups. Scale exercises should also be performed with content from the category list. Material should be performed within comfortable ranges. Singing of tonal patterns, melodies, and harmony parts should be included along with playing instruments. Perform familiar, easy songs without notation using various starting pitches, modes, meters, and articulations so students may focus on accurate, in-tune playing with appropriate tone quality, phrasing, and dynamics.

Acceptable instrumental techniques and accurate ensemble playing should be stressed during warm-ups. Tone quality and production, posture, hand positions, and fingerings need continual attention by performers and instructors. Ensemble concerns of blend, balance, precision, and intonation should also be addressed during warm-up activities. Intonation training is directly related to a sense of tonality, audiation, and correct instrumental techniques. Simple chord progressions and chorales offer much opportunity for musical learning in ensemble rehearsals directed by discerning educator-conductors. Most of these same objectives apply to choral ensemble warm-ups and reinforce that conductors of rehearsals must use their musical skills and teach regardless of type or size of ensemble.

Intonation Training

Performing with acceptable intonation is basically an outgrowth of tonal audiation. Instrumentalists who are trained to sing and play tonal patterns, recognize modes, and hear harmonic function will play in tune because they can *hear* out-of-tuneness. An essential component of good intonation is to audiate melodies and exercises before attempting to perform them on an instrument. If a trumpet student is assigned a tune in G major and returns after a week of practice playing all the F-sharps as F-naturals, this should not be diagnosed as a technique or reading problem, but rather as an audiation problem. Students who correct their own pitch errors are demonstrating the necessary readiness to perform in tune.

Techniques and procedures for tuning should be taught starting in the first month of instruction. Students who are allowed to regularly perform out of tune will learn to accept out-of-tuneness as in-tuneness. Matching individual pitches to tuning notes is useful only for adjusting instruments to approximate pitch areas. Demonstrate the sounds of in-tune and out-of-tune playing by performing a pitch with a student on a wind or stringed instrument. Draw attention to the "beats" sounded when out of tune, and how the faster the "beats," the farther out of tune are the pitches. Pairs of students should practice this technique also. Teach tuning idiosyncrasies of specific instruments as material demands. It is helpful for wind instrumentalists to learn that one way to lower a pitch is to lengthen the tube (lengthen to lower); to raise a pitch, shorten the tube (shorten to sharpen). It is commonly believed that stringed instrument and trombone performers require immediate attention to techniques for playing in tune, but remember that these techniques are of little use without the prerequisite readiness of audiation. The same immediate attention should be given to all students, regardless of instrument played. The teacher's role is to assist in developing musical readiness for the instrument, to teach the necessary technical skills to play in tune, and to avoid doing the tuning for students after initial modeling.

Electronic tuning devices can be helpful to check whether an instrument is generally in tune with a tuning-pitch standard. They are also useful to verify out-of-tuneness on specific pitches that students have accepted as in tune. Keep in mind that tuning individual pitches never guarantees in-tune performance. Electronic tuners are limited for improving intonation during performance; trained ears are the critical tool.

Materials

Lesson materials for beginning instrumentalists should be chosen with tonal and rhythmic patterns in mind. As was mentioned in previous chapters, simple folk songs and general music repertoire are most appropriate. Many teachers rely primarily on trite, contrived exercises

High school clarinet choir in rehearsal

from instrument method books. Good teaching demands finding materials that fit the content objectives. It is not productive to choose a beginning instrument book and follow through it page by page under the assumption that the content is efficiently organized and appropriate for learning.

Choosing beginning method books should include criteria for technical training and musical training. Questions to consider include: Are technical skills introduced in a logical sequence and do they move at a reasonable pace? Are there accurate pictures or illustrations and explanations of hand positions, posture, and embouchure? Is the fingering chart understandable? Are familiar songs included in major, minor, and other modes, in a variety of keys, and in duple and triple meters? Are songs from many sources and cultures? Are lyrics included with songs? Are rhythm and tonal patterns extracted from the songs? Are duets, rounds, harmony lines, and other opportunities for performing parts included? Does the notation accurately represent the rhythmic feel of the songs? Are correct key signatures used?

Students of all levels should work on material that includes independent parts. Ostinatos, harmony lines, combinable sections, partner songs, and rounds are particularly useful in developing independent performers. Many books of ensembles for various small groupings of instruments are available. Class lessons and ensemble rehearsals should include materials to be performed in parts. Early attention to blend, balance, tone quality, intonation, articulations, and rhythmic accuracy then becomes possible.

Sight-reading (Generalization at the Symbolic Association level) materials should be introduced soon after students can read and perform some familiar songs. Unfamiliar songs that include familiar tonal and rhythmic patterns should be chosen for sight-reading material. The author recommends choosing initial material with at least 75 percent familiar patterns. Unfamiliar patterns that students cannot perform should be echoed with correct syllables before attempting them again in notation.

Many publishers of beginning instrumental method books also make available cassette tapes and compact discs that include performances and accompaniments of songs from their books. These recordings can be valuable aids for students, to first hear a version of a given song or to perform with an accompaniment. Performing rhythmically with good intonation and phrasing may be enhanced with their use.

Solo literature and small-ensemble music are integral materials for developing instrumental musicians. Interesting and worthwhile selections are available from the beginning through advanced levels for all instruments and most ensemble combinations. Solo and small-ensemble instruction could become the main musical learning and performance vehicle after beginning-class instruction. The main goal for more advanced instrumentalists is expressive and stylistic interpretation of the literature for their instrument, whether in a solo or ensemble setting.

Students who have developed a tonal and rhythm pattern vocabulary along with instrument facility can generate many of their own materials. Arranging and composing for instrumental classes and ensembles allows students to utilize their musical and instrumental skills in creative and productive ways at the inference level of learning. Students should be encouraged to perform their own compositions and those of their peers.

It is important to have regular use and review of materials that require all fingerings and techniques learned. A variety of keys, modes, and meters in material will aid musical and technical-skill development and help maintain student interest.

As instrumentalist students progress from elementary school through high school and college, ensemble literature shifts from training materials to the standard repertoire. The ensemble music in effect becomes the curriculum in many secondary school instrumental programs. In a survey of one hundred high school band directors, Bauer (1996) found that the primary curricular concern when selecting music for bands is technical demands for performance, and the secondary concern is the cognitive and affective aspects of the music. He suggests that many teachers may select musical compositions first and then derive curricular objectives rather than beginning with their objectives and then choosing music to teach them. This may result in students missing the opportunity to learn important musical knowledge and skills. These priorities could be reversed if careful attention to sequential, organized music training along with instrumental training are the primary organizers of the curriculum.

The beginning emphases of tonal and rhythm vocabulary building, basic musical skills and knowledge, and learning instrument technique gradually shifts to emphasis on musical independence and repertoire building along with expansion and refining of stylistic performance, interpretation, and advanced techniques. As students progress, pattern learning with syllables becomes a secondary focus. Individual musical achievement through instrumental sight-reading, improvisation, arranging, and composition skills should become dominant. With a solid foundation at beginning levels, this transition is achievable by all, and music selections can then be chosen primarily for musical reasons.

Review Questions

1. How do class instruction teaching techniques differ from those used in private lessons?
2. What are some of the executive skills or techniques necessary to perform on oboe?
3. What is the inconsistency between learning-skills sequence and initial instruction of beginning instrumental technique through reading contrived exercises?

4. How does a vocabulary of tonal and rhythm patterns benefit learning to play an instrument?
5. How might rhythm patterns be combined with teaching instrument techniques?
6. How can instrumental techniques be improved through learning transposition?
7. When and how should training begin for musical style, phrasing, dynamics, and form?
8. What are some examples of choices students might make that combine technical and musical skills?
9. How do improvisation and instrument-technique skills interact?
10. What is a benefit of composition activities to learning to perform on an instrument?
11. What is the relationship of technique and musical skills to sight-reading?
12. When is it appropriate to begin sight-reading activities?
13. What is the relationship between diagnostic and prescriptive teaching and content and learning sequences?
14. What should be the next step if a student is unable to play a given tonal pattern on a flash card?
15. What are two basic rules to remember when teaching technical skills?
16. How should students be prepared for home practice?
17. How may rehearsal warm-ups develop instrumental and musical skills?
18. Describe some techniques for intonation training.
19. What are some criteria for choosing materials for beginning instrumentalists?

Assignments

1. Construct a song sheet for use with various instruments following the examples in Figures 5.4 and 5.5.
2. Write out a sequence of technical skills for initially teaching your major-performance instrument.
3. Write out a sequence of technical skills for initially teaching an instrument other than your major-performance instrument.

4. Examine any beginning instrument book. What are the tonal, rhythmic, and instrument-technique sequences?

References

AZZARA, CHRISTOPHER D. (1993). Audiation-based improvisation techniques and elementary instrumental students' music achievement. *Journal of Research in Music Education* 41 (4), 328–342.

BAUER, WILLIAM I. (1996). The selection of concert band music by high school band directors. *Update*, in press.

GARDNER, HOWARD. (1993). *Multiple intelligences: The theory into practice.* New York: Basic Books.

GORDON, EDWIN E. (1993). *Learning sequences in music: Skill, content, and patterns.* Chicago: GIA Publications, Inc.

HOVEY, NILO. (1976). *Efficient rehearsal procedures for school bands.* Elkhart, IN: The Selmer Co.

KRATUS, JOHN. (1994a). Relationships among children's music audiation and their compositional processes and products. *Journal of Research in Music Education* 42 (2), 115–130.

———. (1994b). The ways children compose. *Musical connections: Tradition and change.* Proceedings of the 21st World Conference of the International Society for Music Education, 128–141.

LUCE, J. R. (1965). Sight-reading and ear-playing abilities as related to instrumental music students. *Journal of Research in Music Education* 13, 101–109.

MAINWARING, J. (1941). The meaning of musicianship: A problem in the teaching of music. *British Journal of Educational Psychology* 11 (3), 205–214.

MARK, MICHAEL L. (1996). *Contemporary music education,* 3rd ed. New York: Schirmer Books.

MCPHERSON, GARY E. (1993). Factors and abilities influencing the development of visual, aural and creative performance skills in music and their educational implications. Ph.D. diss., University of Sydney, Australia, DA 54/04-A, 1277. University Microfilms No. 9317278.

———. (1994). Factors and abilities influencing sight-reading skill in music. *Journal of Research in Music Education* 42 (3), 217–231.

MURSELL, JAMES L., and MABELLE GLENN. (1931). *The psychology of music teaching.* New York: Silver Burdett Co.

PRIEST, P. (1989). Playing by ear: Its nature and application to instrumental learning. *British Journal of Music Education* 6 (2), 173–191.

WEBSTER, PETER R. (1990). Creativity as creative thinking. *Music Educators Journal* 76 (9), 22–28.

———. (1994). Thinking in sound: Studying children's improvisation. *Musical connections: Tradition and change.* Proceedings of the 21st World Conference of the International Society for Music Education, 146–153.

WILSON, FRANK R. (1981). Mind, muscle and music: Physiological clues to better teaching. *Teachercraft Bulletin* 4, Elkhart, IN: The Selmer Co.

For Further Reading

Woodwinds

BAINES, ANTHONY. (1963). *Woodwind instruments and their history*, revised ed. New York: W. W. Norton.

PENCE, HOMER. (1963). *Teacher's guide to the bassoon.* Elkhart, IN: The Selmer Co.

PUTNIK, EDWIN. (1970). *The art of flute playing.* Evanston, IL: Summy-Birchard Co.

SPENCER, WILLIAM G. (1969). *The art of bassoon playing*, 2nd ed., revised by Frederick A. Meuller. Evanston, IL: Summy-Birchard Co.

SPRENKLE, ROBERT, and DAVID LEDET. (1961). *The art of oboe playing.* Evanston, IL: Summy-Birchard Co.

STEIN, KEITH. (1958). *The art of clarinet playing.* Evanston, IL: Summy-Birchard Co.

TEAL, LARRY. (1968). *The art of saxophone playing.* Evanston, IL: Summy-Birchard Co.

WESTPHAL, FREDERICK W. (1990). *Guide to teaching woodwinds*, 5th ed. Dubuque, IA: W. C. Brown.

Brasses

BAILEY, WAYNE, et al. (1992). *Teaching brass: A resource manual.* New York: McGraw-Hill.

BAINES, ANTHONY. (1978). *Brass instruments: Their history and development.* New York: Scribner.

FARKAS, PHILIP. (1956). *The art of French horn playing.* Evanston, IL: Summy-Birchard Co.

————. (1962). *The art of brass playing.* Bloomington, IN: Brass Publications.

————. (1976). *The art of musicianship.* Bloomington, IN: Musical Publications.

HUNT, NORMAN, and DAN BACHELDER. (1994). *Guide to teaching brass*, 5th ed. Madison, WI: Brown & Benchmark.

JOHNSON, KEITH. (1981). *The art of trumpet playing.* Ames, IA: Iowa State University Press.

KLEINHAMMER, EDWARD. (1963). *The art of trombone playing.* Evanston, IL: Summy-Birchard Co.

WHITENER, SCOTT. (1990). *A complete guide to brass instruments and pedagogy.* New York: Schirmer.

Strings

GALAMIAN, IVAN. (1962). *Principles of violin playing and teaching.* Englewood Cliffs, NJ: Prentice-Hall, Inc.

GREEN, ELIZABETH A. H. (1966). *Teaching stringed instruments in classes.* Englewood Cliffs, NJ: Prentice-Hall, Inc.

KLOTMAN, ROBERT H. (1996). *Teaching strings*, 2nd ed. New York: Schirmer Books.

KROLICK, EDWARD. (1957). *Basic principles of double bass playing.* Washington, D.C.: Music Educators National Conference.

LAMB, NORMAN, and SUSAN LAMB COOK. (1994). *Guide to teaching strings*, 6th ed. Madison, WI: Brown & Benchmark.

ODDO, VINCENT. (1979). *Playing and teaching the strings.* Belmont, CA: Wadsworth Publishing Co.

POTTER, LOUIS. (1964). *The art of cello playing.* Evanston, IL: Summy-Birchard Co.

Percussion

BLADES, JAMES. (1973). *Orchestral percussion technique*, 2nd ed. London: Oxford
   University Press.
BREITHAUPT, ROBERT. (1991). *The complete percussionist*. Oskaloosa, IA: C.L. Barnhouse.
COOK, GARY D. (1996). *Teaching percussion*, 2nd ed. New York: Schirmer.
HOLLOWAY, RONALD A., and HARRY R. BARTLETT. (1984). *Guide to teaching percus-
   sion*, 4th ed. Dubuque, IA: W. C. Brown Co.

Piano

COLLINS, RICHARD. (1986). *Piano playing: A positive approach*. Lanham, MD: University
   Press of America.
RABIN, RHODA. (1996). *At the beginning: Teaching piano to the very young child*. New York:
   Schirmer Books.
USZLER, MARIENNE, STEWART GORDON, and ELYSE MACH. (1991). *The well-tem-
   pered keyboard teacher*. New York: Schirmer Books.

Music Lists

ANDERSON, PAUL G. (1976). *Brass solo and study material music guide*. Evanston, IL: The
   Instrumentalist Co.
————. (1978). *Brass ensemble music guide*. Evanston, IL: The Instrumentalist Co.
BERGER, KENNETH, ed. *Band music guide*, 9th ed. Evanston, IL: The Instrumentalist Co.
DVORAK, THOMAS, L. (1986). *Best music for young bands*. Brooklyn, NY: Manhattan
   Beach.
GRECHESKY, ROBERT, and GARY M. CIEPLUCH. (1993). *Best music for high school band*.
   Brooklyn, NY: Manhattan Beach.
LONDEIX, JEAN MARIE. (1985). *Music for saxophone: General repertoire of music and edu-
   cational literature for saxophone*. New York: Roncorp.
MAYER, FREDERICK R., ed. (1993). *The string orchestra super list*. Reston, VA: Music
   Educators National Conference.
NATIONAL BAND ASSOCIATION. (1990). *Selective music list for bands: 1990 revision*.
SCHLEUTER, STANLEY L. (1993). *Saxophone recital music: A discography*. Westport, CT:
   Greenwood Press.
VOXMAN, HIMIE, and LYLE MERRIMAN. (1982). *Woodwind music, guide: Ensemble music
   in print*. Evanston, IL: The Instrumentalist Co.
————. (1982). *Woodwind solo and study material guide*. Evanston, IL: The Instrumentalist Co.

Improvisation Materials

AEBERSOLD, JAMEY. (1971–1995). *A new approach to jazz improvisation*. New Albany, IN:
   Jamey Aebersold.
FROSETH, JAMES O. (1988). *Aural skills training series: Advanced studies in ear-to-hand fin-
   ger pattern technique*. Chicago: GIA Publications, Inc.
SCHMID, WILL. (1985). *Jazz/rock trax*. Milwaukee: Hal Leonard Publishing.

Instrumental Music Teaching Techniques

CASEY, JOSEPH L. (1993). *Teaching techniques and insights for instrumental music educators, revised.* Chicago: GIA Publications, Inc.

GAROFALO, ROBERT J. (1992). *Guides for band masterworks.* Fort Lauderdale, FL: Meredith Music Publications.

LABUTA, JOSEPH A. (1972). *Teaching musicianship in the high school band.* West Nyack, NY: Parker Publishing Co.

LISK, EDWARD S. (1991). *The creative director: Alternative rehearsal techniques,* 3rd ed. Fort Lauderdale, FL: Meredith Music Publications.

Teaching examples: Ideas for music educators. (1994). Reston, VA: Music Educators National Conference.

CHAPTER 6

Some Aspects of the Teaching Process

In order for learning to occur, how we teach students is as important as what and why we teach. Teaching practices are varied and diverse for music as well as for other subjects. During the past three decades or so, researchers have investigated many aspects of the teaching/learning process, and new insights have evolved along with confirmation of many of the traditional teaching techniques. Although most of the research has occurred with non-music students and teachers, there is an increasing number of studies specific to music teaching. There is also increased interest by music researchers in the studies outside the music field that may be applicable to music situations.

Effective teaching is a very complex process and depends on a number of variables. Teacher personality, intelligences, aptitudes, musical skill and knowledge levels, expectations, communication skills, and values are examples of some of the variables that combine to influence student achievement. Groupings of students may differ dramatically from year to year with regard to amount of structure needed, behavior patterns, and motivation to learn. Not everyone teaches effectively, and there are no simple recipes for teachers to follow or to help in training teachers. At least with instrumental music, it may be claimed that if you can't teach, you can always play.

A variety of aspects must be combined and balanced for the teaching process to be effective. The limited number of topics selected for this chapter are particularly germane to teaching instrumental music and are gathered from a variety of sources. The intent is to present information to help all teachers, beginners through experienced, in refining their approach to teaching instrumental music and music in general. The first sections of this chapter draw upon syntheses of general-education research on topics of explicit/implicit learning, modeling, transfer, and motivation. An important goal for teachers is to make themselves dispensable by enabling their students to learn independently. Effective teaching is concerned with organizing instruction, motivating students, and facilitating how students transfer knowledge and skills. The remainder of the chapter presents additional teaching suggestions that are based on a synthesis of research in music education and are directly applicable to music teaching. The occasional overlap in content that occurs among the various syntheses corroborates the complexity of the teaching/learning process and the interrelationships of its various aspects.

An Overview

An examination of the relationships of teaching and student achievement across various content areas and age levels produces some worthwhile information for music teaching practices. Some general observations from a comprehensive literature review by Brophy and Good (1986) include that student learning is greatly influenced by the amount of time spent on a task, and that learning is more efficient when teachers structure the tasks, help to relate to what is known, monitor student performance, and provide feedback. These five observations are easily applied to teaching music.

Porter and Brophy (1988, p. 75) reviewed effective teaching research across age levels and content areas and concluded that effective teachers

- are clear about their instructional goals
- are knowledgeable about their content and the strategies for teaching it
- communicate to their students what is expected of them—and why
- make expert use of existing instructional materials in order to devote more time to practices that enrich and clarify the content
- are knowledgeable about their students, adapting instruction to their needs and anticipating misconceptions in their existing knowledge
- teach students metacognitive strategies and give them opportunities to master them
- address higher- as well as lower-level cognitive objectives

- monitor students' understanding by offering regular appropriate feedback
- integrate their instruction with that in other subject areas
- accept responsibility for student outcomes
- are thoughtful and reflective about their practice.

Reread the above list and think about how it applies to music teachers you have experienced or to your own teaching. Much of the list, if not all, should appear to be common sense, but upon reflection and analysis it is surprising how often teachers ignore some of the basics of teaching.

In a synthesis of mainly descriptive music-education research, Brand (1985, pp. 13–16) suggests that effective music teachers

> tend to be extroverted, enthusiastic, and sincerely care for their students. As expected, the students in these successful music teachers' classes actively participate and show interest and enjoyment. Competencies that characterize effective teachers include (1) musicianship, particularly skill in diagnosing and correcting musical errors and the use of the voice in demonstrating performance techniques; (2) skill in classroom and rehearsal management; and (3) the ability to relate lesson objectives to students' interests and needs.

Organizing and Presenting Instruction

There are many ways to organize and present instrumental music instruction. Teachers need criteria and structure to base their decisions upon for choosing techniques most appropriate for individual learners. Learning is facilitated by various amounts and types of structure. Again, research from the areas of education, psychology, and music education provides us with valuable assistance in devising effective teaching strategies.

Implicit and Explicit Learning

One way to look at the complex music-learning process is to label and classify it as implicit and explicit learning—categories often found in psychological research. Implicit learning refers to what is learned without direct instruction in an unconscious, usually unstructured, and automatic manner. An example is the songs children learn on their own, which might include not only the melody and rhythms but also style, dynamics, vocal inflections, and movements. Implicit learning is particularly common with children before they enter school and is perhaps best exemplified by their language acquisition. Initial perception of rhythm and pitch, production through singing, and playing by ear are mainly learned implicitly. Teachers can facilitate implicit learning through nondirected modeling such as playing recordings of music of particular styles and instrumentations and performing for their students.

Explicit learning usually starts with verbal instruction to a learner who then attempts to achieve the task. Much instrumental learning is based on explicit instructions such as, "Hold your fingers like this. Now take a breath and blow a fast stream of air." Unlike implicit learning, explicit learning is dependent on structure and organization of content. Most of the tonal and rhythm-pattern learning discussed in Chapters 3–5 is an example of explicit learning. It is not always clear to what degree some things are learned implicitly or explicitly, because of individual learning differences. Explicit learning is the focus when teachers give directed verbal instruction and demonstrations. When teaching students how to play instruments, decide which tasks might best be approached through implicit or explicit learning. It is recommended that teachers be sensitive to their students' needs and encourage implicit learning whenever possible and use explicit learning as necessary to complete the learning tasks.

Cziko (1988, p. 105) makes suggestions for music teachers to facilitate explicit and implicit learning and recommends that implicit and explicit learning be integrated through a synthesis-analysis-synthesis approach. Initially for synthesis, emphasize implicit learning through techniques such as providing ample opportunity for students to hear live and recorded music that includes content you wish to emphasize. Teach explicitly those tasks that students did not grasp implicitly, and lastly, emphasize synthesis through implicit learning by combining components into a musical whole.

Modeling and Demonstration

Instrumental teachers tend to use verbal instruction much of the time. High school band rehearsals have been shown to contain up to 42 percent of teacher talk (Pontius, 1982). With regard to instrumental-music teaching, verbal instruction is far less effective than modeling and demonstration. We know that students of all ages can benefit from appropriate teacher modeling and can improve their performances. In a later study, Dickey (1991) found that middle school band classes demonstrated greater ear-to-hand skills and kinesthetic response skills when provided teacher modeling than did classes that provided verbal instruction only. After studying the quality and amount of modeling used by teachers of beginning instrumentalists, Sang (1987) concludes that teachers who have stronger modeling skills and apply those skills are more likely to produce students with higher performance achievement than teachers who do not.

Teacher modeling is usually provided through singing or performing on an instrument, but the use of recordings is also strongly recommended. Quality recordings can serve as the Aural/Oral basis for students to develop audiation skills. For example, the Suzuki approach to teaching strings makes extensive use of recorded models of music to be performed by students. Providing practice tapes for students is also productive and is supported in studies by Puopolo (1971), Zurcher (1975), Carroll (1987), and others.

Teacher modeling for students

Modeling may be explicit or implicit instruction, as mentioned above. Students may be explicitly directed to watch or listen to a specific teacher model or demonstration before or after attempting a given task. It is also useful to occasionally provide incorrect models along with correct models so that students may compare and contrast. This also helps train student critiquing skills. Implicit modeling occurs when students might observe or hear teacher demonstration without attention directed to the model. Of course, any teacher modeling or demonstration must be performed *accurately* for students to respond appropriately.

Education researchers have examined the relationship of teaching process with resulting student achievement. These correlation studies are often called process-product research, and although the results may not be interpreted as the process actually causing the product, the number of studies with similar findings provides strong evidence of the relationships. Most of the studies used elementary and junior high school students in non-music subjects but are applicable to explicit, systematic teaching of structured content. For example, Rosenshine and Stevens (1986) provide a general model of six basic instructional functions with details listed for each function. A study by Taebel and Coker (1980) is an example of the few studies of this type that are specific to music.

Transfer

Tranfer is the ability to utilize what is known or familiar in unknown or unfamiliar circumstances. Everything we do and learn is influenced by previous knowledge and experiences. Most music teachers have worked with students who were able to generalize to new situations without assistance. Teachers learn that the assumption transfer takes place is frequently proven wrong when students require reteaching of a concept or skill nearly every time a new context occurs. Studies confirm that transfer does not occur in the majority of situations, and that teachers can facilitate its occurrence through certain presentation practices.

Much research exists in education and psychology on transfer. The current thinking generally emphasizes cognitive theories and a mix of behavioristic and cognitive concepts. One of the most recent and comprehensive synthesis of transfer research with applications to music teaching was written by Shuell (1988) and Edwards (1988) in their chapters in *The Crane Symposium*. Within their discussions and interpretations of studies, they make suggestions for music teachers to help transfer occur. Shuell (p. 149) believes that the ultimate goal of educational experiences in music is transfer. He states that transfer is allowed to occur when students have actually learned, not when teachers think students have learned.

Edwards (pp. 131, 135, 138) provides additional suggestions and specifics for transfer in music learning:

- All transfer is not automatic; make your students musical thinkers, not musical robots
- Use verbal labels ("conceptual pegs") to help students store away musical ideas and see relationships between musical situations
- In general, attach labels after the phenomenon has been experienced
- Since auditory models may not be retained in memory well enough for later use, be prepared to sharpen the memory by repeating the model
- Verbalize often, but be brief and to the point
- Developing too many skills at one time results in confusion; break complex problems into component parts to achieve mastery
- Componenting can be overdone, however; too much of it may stifle integration and development of a good final product
- Slow practice does not suddenly transfer to rapid, accurate performance; have students "shape" difficult passages, gradually bringing them up to tempo
- In teaching specific musical tasks, teach students the "why" of what you want; for example, relate "louder" and "softer" to ensemble balance
- Students tend to see learning in bits and pieces and miss the "big picture"; keep students informed about how their individual work relates to the final product
- Encourage students to develop the habit of distributed rather than concentrated practice; it is more effective
- Treat technique books as transfer exercises based on common musical patterns and situations—they are not magical routes to total musicianship
- To develop musical thinking and maximize transfer, make students apply what they have learned elsewhere to the situation at hand

- Use demonstration frequently; add just enough verbalization to focus on the salient point
- Sight-reading is a skill that can be developed through practice
- Let students know that mental practice is beneficial and thus a legitimate way of learning; injury should not be a valid excuse to miss a lesson or rehearsal

Careful study of the above suggestions will assist the reader in transfer of content from Chapters 3–5 in this book into the context of teaching. For example, when applying Gordon's learning skills sequence to tonal and rhythm pattern learning, transfer is what occurs when the learner moves from the Discrimination levels to the Inference levels. A unique feature of the learning skills sequence is the use of Verbal Association syllables to aurally label patterns and serve as "verbal pegs." The tonal and rhythm syllables facilitate transfer of familiar patterns to unfamiliar contexts, first without notation, later with notation. Interested readers are urged to examine the chapters by Shuell and Edwards for the detailed discussion and citings leading to the above list of suggestions.

Other suggestions to facilitate transfer for instrumental students include regular use of Partial Synthesis and Composite Synthesis teaching techniques as discussed in previous chapters. It is also helpful to use analogies as part of verbal instructions. Check for levels of student understanding and skills often, and do not assume that instructions are understood.

Motivation

Student motivation is a critical component of the teaching-learning process and is the subject of thousands of studies and articles in the field of education. The study of why students pursue certain interests and goals with energy and persistence is helpful for teachers because it is an area that we may influence to some extent. There are a number of schools of thought concerning motivation theories. Most are involved in one way or another with extrinsic motivation (motivating factors from outside the person) and intrinsic motivation (motivating factors from within the person). Behaviorists dwell on outside motivators such as rewards, punishment, and reinforcers. Humanistic approaches center around personal fulfillment and needs. Cognitivists emphasize how we explore meaning, understanding, and individual beliefs. Others emphasize the importance of valuing goals and expectation levels for success. Most teachers operate with a mixture of motivation beliefs and techniques when working with their students, and most students are motivated by a variety of sources.

Teachers need to observe individual preferences, aptitudes, attitudes, and backgrounds of students, and assign learning tasks that are challenging but not overwhelming. Clearly stated objectives and goals with criteria for achievement are essential for students to develop feelings of success, confidence, and self-esteem. Teacher expectation of students is a critical factor. Students need to believe that they can improve their performance and not limit their efforts by avoiding possible failure. When achievement is expected and encouraged, success is promoted. It is true that success breeds success; however, failure may also be a positive motivator, especially with intrinsically motivated tasks. Parental involvement and support of student efforts is also

Guitarist improving a solo in jazz ensemble rehearsal

important. Zdzinski (1992) maintains that parental support influences attitudes and motivation of instrumental students.

Music teachers often use extrinsic motivators ranging from gold stars, stickers, and pins, to trips to Florida. Over time, however, extrinsic motivation is not as useful as intrinsic motivation for school learners. Stipek (1986, p. 203) states that

- continuous use of rewards has negative long-term effects because of constant need for rewards to continue desired learning behavior; and
- student cognitions, beliefs, and values are more important in determining achievement behavior than reinforcement.

Others such as Ryan, Connell, and Deci (1985) contend that external motivators may lower student self-concept because they have less control over the learning task.

A number of studies about motivation and music education have recently appeared, including those by Asmus (1986, 1989), Austin (1988), Austin and Vispoel (1992), and Vispoel (1994). The role of attributions is of particular interest in accounting for a portion of student motivation. Attribution theory relates to the reasons given by students for their successes and failures and assumes these reasons will influence future performance. Effort and musical ability are the main attributes to which students attribute success or failure. A promising model of music-achievement motivation is proposed by Asmus (1994). He connects the influences of self-perceptions, attributions, teaching strategies, music materials, and social value to music learning. Asmus maintains that about 20 percent of achievement is due to student motivation, and that intrinsic motives are most important to develop in students through teaching strategies, feedback, and the learning situation.

There is general agreement that feedback, including praise, is valuable for motivation. Students need timely information about what they are doing well in particular. This is when confirmed success begins to motivate future successes. Brophy (1981, p. 32) did an extensive review of research concerning teacher praise. He points out that praise has differing purposes and meanings, depending on context, and that *quality* of teacher praise is more consequential than *frequency* of use. His suggestions for effective teacher praise are listed in Table 6.1.

Table 6.1   GUIDELINES FOR EFFECTIVE PRAISE

EFFECTIVE PRAISE	INEFFECTIVE PRAISE
1. is delivered contingently	1. is delivered randomly or unsystematically
2. specifies the particulars of the accomplishment	2. is restricted to global positive reactions
3. shows spontaneity, variety, and other signs of credibility	3. shows a bland uniformity that suggests a conditioned response
4. rewards attainment of specified performance criteria (which can include effort criteria, however)	4. rewards mere participation without consideration of performance processes or outcomes
5. provides information to students about their competence or the value of their accomplishments	5. provides no information at all or gives students information about their status
6. orients students toward better appreciation of their own task-related behavior and thinking about problem solving	6. orients students toward comparing themselves with others and thinking about competing
7. uses students' own prior accomplishments as the context for describing present accomplishments	7. uses the accomplishments of peers as the context for describing students' present accomplishments
8. is given in recognition of noteworthy effort or success at difficult (for this student) tasks	8. is given without regard to the effort expended or the meaning of the accomplishment
9. attributes success to effort and ability, implying that similar successes can be expected in the future	9. attributes success to ability alone or to external factors such as luck or low task difficulty
10. fosters endogenous attributions (students believe that they expend effort on the task because they enjoy the task and/or want to develop task-relevant skills)	10. fosters exogenous attributions (students believe that they expend effort on the task for external reasons—to please the teacher, win a competition or reward, etc.)
11. focuses students' attention on their own task-relevant behavior	11. focuses students' attention on the teacher as an external authority figure who is manipulating them
12. fosters an appreciation of and desirable attributions about task-relevant behavior after the process is completed	12. intrudes into the ongoing process, distracting attention from task-relevant behavior

Positive feedback mixed with occasional constructive criticism is a powerful student motivator in lessons, classes, and rehearsals.

Suggestions for Teaching Music Performance

The material in this section is taken from Schleuter and Schleuter (1988), Chapter 6 of *The Crane Symposium*. These suggestions are taken from the portions of that chapter concerned with the research implications for how and when we might effectively teach and learn music performance. Many aspects of music performance have been studied. The amount of research on each topic varies, and the intent here is to synthesize the implications rather than cite and discuss specific studies. Much of the material is directly related to information previously presented in this book, and many of these suggestions should not be new information to the reader. One of the most useful purposes of music-performance research is to confirm and refine procedures that are already in use. The teaching suggestions below may be helpful in rethinking or reaffirming emphases and expanding the objectives of how you teach.

1. Encourage productive student practicing through developing clear goals.

It should not be assumed that learners automatically know how to practice effectively. Efficient practice routines are learned. It is best to help the learner get in mind the desired musical results and to set short-term and long-term performance goals. Musical goals should be emphasized that are attainable and appropriate for the learner.

2. Stress the importance of quality and quantity of repetition.

Repetition of sections of music is an efficient process for learning performance skills and is increasingly necessary as the music becomes more complicated and long. The ability to isolate repeated sections increases with awareness of structure in the music and is an indicator of increasing skill level. Quality of repetition may be as important as quantity—careful practice with clear goals is most effective.

3. Encourage short, distributed practice sessions rather than few long sessions.

Nearly fifty years of studies in psychology and music indicate that music is learned more easily in distributed, shorter practice or rehearsal periods over time than in fewer, longer practice sessions. This has obvious implications for school performance group rehearsals, music classes, and home practice—instruct beginners to practice two or three times daily for short periods rather than one long session, and spread rehearsals over time in reasonable, short periods of concentrated activity.

4. Provide specific feedback regularly to students about performance results.

Performance feedback occurs in various forms and is necessary for the learner to form correct habits through repetition by confirming results with intent. A common example is teacher critiques during training sessions. Learner self-feedback while performing may be most effective when comparing one's performance to an internalized model of the music (audiation). If the learner is unsure of what the end product should be, it is difficult to provide meaningful self-feedback.

5. Help students develop internalized models of sound by providing live and/or recorded models.

Numerous studies demonstrate that providing a model of sound for students to imitate and conceptualize the desired effect is an important technique in efficient practice and performance of music. Either live or recorded examples are useful. Music-teaching approaches by Suzuki and the Manhattanville Music Curriculum Project are two examples that emphasize models of sound. Tape recorders are greatly under-utilized as a means to provide models of sound and for self-assessment with music-performance learning. Nearly everyone has access to a cassette tape recorder. Teachers can help students have another music reason to utilize the "boom box."

6. Have students practice at slower tempi and gradually increase speed to develop rapid technique.

Motor skills and musical performance are interdependent and are related to rhythmic response and to performance skill techniques for manipulating musical instruments. Studies indicate that proficiency of music motor skills increases with age and that girls do better than boys in primary grades.

Studies of human brain function and the neurological system with relation to music performance and learning indicate that rapid instrumental technique is attained through slow practice with a goal of live performance. Doing it right the first time through is a meaningful goal.

There is evidence that when slowing tempi for practice, it is best not to slow to the point where the location of the underlying tempo beats is altered.

7. Develop instrumental technique with melodic material and solo literature rather than primarily drill exercises.

Young learners of instruments are more motivated to practice melodic material than to drill on contrived exercises. Emphasizing musical, melodic material and solo literature is preferable to technique drills such as long tones, scales, and arpeggios for beginning performers. Many music teachers do use primarily melodic material, and this approach was advocated sixty years ago by writers such as James Mursell and others before him. An implication is that we should not send students home with mainly drill and contrived exercises and expect them to practice.

8. Provide opportunities for students to audiate music notation when practicing and performing.

Audiation is what occurs when one thinks through a melody of a familiar song or when one looks at music notation and "hears" it. Facility with audiation is important to a performer and is trainable. Mental preparation for performance appears to be an effective technique. The best sight-readers appear to audiate what is to be performed. A possible teaching technique example is to ask instrumental students to carefully "sing your music in your head while doing the fingerings." Singers might be asked to "sing the music silently" before singing aloud.

9. Motivate students in beginning levels with external rewards, including approval from parents, teachers, and peers; competitions; and recitals.

Young students are motivated to practice through extrinsic rewards such as awards, recitals, competitions, and even gold stars. Approval and encouragement from peers, parents, and teachers is also an effective motivator. As students progress through years of training, they should have opportunities to become more self-motivating.

10. Require and expect students to commit much time, effort, and self-responsibility to achieve professional levels of performance through years of preparation.

If you have students who desire to perform professionally, it is important to know that the most essential ingredient is probably the amount of time and effort they expend toward their performance goals. This is most likely equally or more important than their music aptitude.

11. Use group or individual settings to provide performance instruction.

Many music teachers assume that individual instruction is more effective than group instruction. We all know that the majority of studio teachers teach one student at a time while the majority of school instruction is with groups of varying sizes. The few studies on this topic found no achievement differences between individual or group instruction for beginning students. Motivation to learn and teacher behaviors are probably more important than the setting.

12. Avoid scheduling student lessons during their classes, but recognize that removing students from school classes for weekly lessons does not significantly lower their academic achievement.

How instruction for instrumental performance is scheduled in elementary schools is occasionally an important concern of educators and parents. Studies indicate that reading, language, and math scores do not suffer when elementary instrumental students are excused from classes for their lessons.

13. Aid memorization of music by increasing awareness of patterns and form and a "whole-part-whole" approach.

Music performers often wish or are required to perform without the written score. Recognizing patterns of tonal, rhythmic, and form configurations aids memorization. Developing a sense of the entirety of a composition or movement and then analyzing its various parts and patterns and how they relate to the whole appear to be most beneficial. Other memorization aids include distributed practice and audiation as mentioned earlier.

14. Encourage students to improvise as a means to experience music at a more personal level.

Most music learners are capable of some level of improvisation skills, and these skills are a valuable means for performers to enjoy music on a more personal level. In the few studies on the topic, improvisation training of elementary through high school instrumentalists resulted in higher achievement levels than of those without such training. Adults who continue to play instruments rate improvisation and sight-reading as most important skills.

15. Recognize that children acquire music performance skills gradually and appear to progress through stages of maturation and development.

Children undergo many gradual mental and physical changes from infancy to adulthood. The changes include the ability to conceptualize and generalize music content and the ability to control motor skills for music performance. Teachers need to develop awareness of developmental stages in learners and diagnostic/prescriptive teaching skills.

16. Adjust content and experiences as children progress through levels of abilities.

Music content must be adapted to the learning level of the child in order for it to be meaningful. An example of typical misuse is teaching college music-theory content to students before they have developed musical readiness. In general, children should experience music through singing, listening, and movement experiences before structured music content is taught.

17. Teach tonal and rhythm pattern vocabularies aurally followed by labeling and notation, regardless of age level.

Acquiring music literacy appears to parallel acquisition of literacy in language. This suggests that children label sound patterns verbally and then learn to recognize the symbols associated with those sounds. Movable *do* syllables are an example of labels that may be effectively used with tonal patterns prior to the introduction of notation.

18. Determine the small steps that will result in the achievement of a particular performance task or skill.

Analyzing the ingredients of music-performance tasks is essential to effective teaching. Complex performance skills are developed through incremental steps. Little research exists to support any one specific model. This means that music teachers must use observation and common sense along with the extant research to help determine appropriate segmenting of "parts" of the musical "whole."

19. Present instruction in small steps in prerequisite order.

Once the learning tasks are determined, careful attention should be given to placing them in prerequisite order. Teachers who get results are often adept at determining when and in what order to introduce new tasks and musical content within the specific grasp of learners. Sequences for tonal and rhythm pattern content appear in Chapters 3 and 4. Instruments are often taught with specific executive skill sequences, however most are not researched with regard to efficacy.

20. Begin students on instruments when both musical and physical readiness are established.

Although it is generally believed that instrumental study should begin during childhood years, no optimum age has been ascertained as the best time to start instruction. Physical size and motor skill development are important, and some studies indicate that fine muscle coordination may be more easily trained prior to adulthood. The age of the learner may not be as important as the quality of instruction and the amount of practice. Students with musical readiness have musical reasons to perform on an instrument that increase motivation and expressive performance.

Review Questions

1. What are the five general observations relating to teaching and student achievement?
2. List some specific characteristics of effective teachers that are found across content areas.
3. What is the role of implicit learning?
4. What is the role of explicit learning?
5. What is the importance of teacher modeling?
6. List at least eight teaching suggestions for facilitating transfer in music learning.
7. What is the role of intrinsic motivation and how might it be encouraged?
8. How does attribution theory relate to motivating music learners?
9. What are some of the ways praise may be used effectively as a motivator?
10. What music-teaching suggestions can you discuss that are supported from research studies?

References

ASMUS, EDWARD P., JR. (1986). Student beliefs about the causes of success and failure in music: A study of achievement motivation. *Journal of Research in Music Education* 34 (4), 262–278.

————. (1989). The effect of music teachers on students' motivation to achieve in music. *Canadian Journal of Research in Music Education* 30, 14–21.

————. (1994). Motivation in music teaching and learning. *The Quarterly* 5 (4), 5–32.

AUSTIN, JAMES R. (1988). The effect of music contest format on self-concept, motivation, achievement, and attitude of elementary band students. *Journal of Research in Music Education* 36 (2), 95–107.

————, and WALTER P. VISPOEL. (1992). Motivation after failure in school music performance classes: The facilitative effects of strategy attributions. *Bulletin of the Council for
Research in Music Education* 111, 1–23.

BRAND, MANNY. (1985). Research in music teacher effectiveness. *Update* 3 (2), 13–16.

BROPHY, JERE. (1981). Teacher praise: A functional analysis. *Review of Educational
Research* 51, 5–32.

————, and THOMAS L. GOOD. (1986). Teacher behavior and student achievement. In
M. Wittrock, ed., *Handbook of research on teaching*, 3rd ed. New York: Macmillan,
328–375.

CARROLL, DONALD. (1987). Development and evaluation of a programmed-like text
with accompanying audio cassette tapes as an ancillary to elementary beginning snare
drum classes. *Contributions to Music Education* 14, 1–8.

CZIKO, GARY. (1988). Implicit and explicit learning: Implications for and applications to
music teaching. Chapter 7 in *The Crane Symposium: Toward an Understanding of the
Teaching and Learning of Music Performance*. Charles Fowler, ed. Potsdam, NY: SUNY
Potsdam.

DICKEY, MARC R. (1991). A comparison of verbal instruction and nonverbal teacher-stu-
dent modeling in instrumental ensembles. *Journal of Research in Music Education* 39 (2),
132–142.

EDWARDS, ROGER. (1988). Transfer and performance instruction. Chapter 8 in *The
Crane Symposium: Toward an Understanding of the Teaching and Learning of Music
Performance*. Charles Fowler, ed. Potsdam, NY: SUNY Potsdam.

PONTIUS, MELVIN F. (1982). A profile of rehearsal techniques and interaction of selected
band conductors. Ph.D. diss., University of Illinois.

PORTER, ANDREW C. and JERE BROPHY. (1988). Synthesis of research on good teaching: Insights from the work of the Institute for Research on Teaching. *Educational
Leadership* 45(8), 74–85.

PUOPOLO, VITO. (1971). The development and experimental application of self-instruc-
tional practice materials for beginning instrumentalists. *Journal of Research in Music
Education* 19 (3), 342–349.

ROSENSHINE, BARAK, and ROBERT STEVENS. (1986). Teaching functions. Chapter
13 in Merlin C. Wittrock, ed. *Handbook of Research on Teaching*, 3rd ed. New York:
Macmillan.

RYAN, R. M., J. P. CONNELL, and E. L. DECI. (1985). A motivational analysis of self-
determination and self-regulation in education. In C. Ames and R. Ames, eds. *Research
on Motivation in Education* 2. San Diego: Academic Press, 13–51.

SANG, RICHARD C. (1987). A study of the relationship between instrumental music
teachers' modeling skills and pupil performance behaviors. *Bulletin of the Council for
Research in Music Education* 91, 155–159.

SCHLEUTER, STANLEY, and LOIS SCHLEUTER. (1988). Teaching and learning music
performance: What, when, and how. Chapter 6 in *The Crane Symposium: Toward an
Understanding of the Teaching and Learning of Music Performance*. Charles Fowler, ed.
Potsdam, NY: SUNY Potsdam, 63–88.

SHUELL, THOMAS. (1988). The role of transfer in the learning and teaching of music: A cognitive perspective. Chapter 9 in *The Crane Symposium: Toward an Understanding of the Teaching
and Learning of Music Performance*. Charles Fowler, ed. Potsdam, NY: SUNY Potsdam.

STIPEK, D. J. (1986). Children's motivation to learn. In T. M. Tomlinson and H. J. Walberg,
eds. *Academic Work and Educational Excellence: Raising Student Productivity*. Berkeley, CA:
McCutchan.

TAEBEL, DONALD K., and JOAN G. COKER. (1980). Teaching effectiveness in elementary classroom music: Relationships among competency measures, pupil product measures, and certain attribute variables. *Journal of Research in Music Education* 28 (4), 250–264.

VISPOEL, WALTER P. (1994). Integrating self-perceptions of music skill into contemporary models of self-concept. *The Quarterly* 5 (4), 42–57.

ZDZINSKI, STEPHEN F. (1992). Relationships among parental involvement and affective outcomes in instrumental music. *Southeastern Journal of Music Education* 4, 155–163.

ZURCHER, WILLIAM. (1975). The effect of model-supportive practice on beginning brass instrumentalists. In C. Madsen, R. D. Greer, and C. H. Madsen, eds. *Research in Music Behavior: Modifying Music Behavior in the Classroom*. New York: Teachers College Press. 131–138.

CHAPTER 7

Assessment of Music Achievement and Music Aptitude

The primary purpose of schools is to promote cognitive learning, which includes perception, conception, and intuition. The music-learning process should result in acquiring knowledge and skills. When instrumental music is included in school curricula, it should be expected that music knowledge and skills are reinforced and acquired through the use of musical instruments. Musical knowledge and skills become the objectives of the instrumental music program and also become the basis for evaluation. If musical objectives are important enough to teach, and if this teaching results in observable student outcomes, measurement is possible and necessary.

Many teachers of school instrumental music, especially at junior high school and high school levels, concentrate on ensemble rather than individual achievement. One reason for this is that school music programs and teachers are often evaluated by how well the instrumental groups rate at contests and competitions rather than how well each student performs and how much each knows about music. Experienced teachers know that high-quality performances of large ensembles can be achieved even when a number of the ensemble members have limited musical knowledge and understanding along with technique deficits. Ensemble results are important and should be evaluated but are difficult to measure objectively. Objective measurement consists of data that are systematically collected with every effort made to eliminate bias and subjectivity. When more than one person scores or rates a test or performance and the result is the same score or rating for students, measurement is basically objective. Contest ratings are often examples of evaluation with limited or subjective measurement when different adjudicators arrive at different ratings upon hearing the same performance. We need to go beyond evaluation based mainly on limited measurement of group results in order to assess how each individual within the group is achieving. Evaluation without adequate objective measurement is of questionable use.

Systematic measurement of individual music achievement of instrumentalists is necessary and desirable for a number of reasons. Probably the most important reason is to assess student progress. Music achievement levels of students need frequent assessment so that appropriate choices of content, materials, and learning levels can be made. Assignment of new tasks should depend upon completion of prerequisite tasks. Instrumental music students whose assignments consist of moving through a method book from page one consecutively to the end and then beginning the next book are not being diagnosed or taught effectively. Students who are only taught in large groups or ensembles need regular assignments to demonstrate knowledge and performance skill that can be measured individually. Diagnostic and prescriptive teaching depends on objective measurement.

Teachers need to report music achievement regularly to students and parents, and objective measurement is essential for valid reports. Reporting music achievement must consist of more than a letter grade for music; it should include an evaluation of performance skills and objectives, a diagnosis of problem areas, and a prescription for continuing improvement. Evaluation is most helpful when based on objective measurement in that instrumental music teachers may evaluate their own effectiveness through the achievements of their students. Student achievement levels also directly reflect on the overall success of the total program.

Systematic assessment of music aptitude (potential to achieve musically) is also desirable. Aptitude test results are important for diagnosis of musical strengths and weaknesses and for identifying talented students before training occurs. Low music aptitude test scores should never be a basis for denying instrumental instruction to students. High music aptitude scores are an indication that a student may profit from instrumental music instruction.

Evaluation is the process of making judgments based on collected data, and measurement is the process of collecting that data. For evaluation to be meaningful, measurement should be objective and systematic; for evaluation to be useful, data must be interpreted and reported in some meaningful form. This implies providing students, parents, and administrators with specifics of musical and technique objectives and how well each student is achieving the objectives.

This chapter will describe the measurement and evaluation of instrumental music achievement and music aptitude. The discussion of objectives for instrumental music achievement will include achievement outcomes for musical knowledge and skills. Measurement of the tonal and rhythmic content described in previous chapters will focus on the musical component. This chapter will also include objectives and measurement techniques pertaining to the development of instrumental performance technique. Teacher-constructed rating scales are presented and discussed in some detail. Selected standardized tests for music achievement and for music aptitude are also discussed. The chapter closes with an example of an instrumental music progress report.

Measuring Instrumental Music Achievement

Measuring music achievement requires clearly understood objectives. Specific examples will appear later in this chapter. The result of teaching carefully planned objectives should be measurable outcomes. Unless both teacher and student understand what the objectives are, measurement is meaningless. Sequential lists of content objectives are most helpful in structuring the teaching and learning processes. The content objectives become the basis for measuring and reporting achievement. The interaction of learning sequence and content may be stated in objectives by including what is being learned and how students demonstrate their achievement. Performance and nonperformance objectives should be stated and measured. The National Standards as listed in Chapter 1 may serve as a basis for organizing objectives and measurement. It is important to use a variety of measurement techniques in order to obtain the clearest possible picture of student achievement.

Instrumental music teachers often do not take the time necessary to measure student achievement objectively. Many teachers have had little or no training in development or use of measurement tools. School instrumental teachers often think primarily of the achievement levels of large performing groups rather than of the individuals within the groups. They ignore objective measurement of individual musical and skill achievement. In many junior and senior high school instrumental programs, the curriculum content is the list of selections prepared for various performances throughout a school year. No systematic, sequential music learning is planned and implemented for the students, so the result is limited opportunity to assess individual musical progress in knowledge and skills.

Instrumental music teachers often get in trouble with program accountability when grades are based primarily on attendance and/or student attitude. The message sent to students, parents, and administrators when attendance is the criteria for a music grade is that showing up is what is important, not what is demonstrated or known musically. Subjective assessment of student attitudes has no place in the measurement process; poor student attitudes are often the result of ineffective teaching. Subjects other than music would soon lose their credibility in the curriculum if similar procedures were also employed for determining grades. There are many ways to assess instrumental music achievement systematically. It is essential that teachers learn how to measure objectively and consistently.

During the past decade or so, a growing interest in alternative assessment (also called performance assessment, authentic assessment, and direct assessment) has developed. Much of this interest is generated as a backlash to standardized tests comprised of multiple-choice items that are widely used to measure academic achievement in subjects other than music. There is also a desire to assess students more directly in all subject areas by focusing on student performance along with products and process. Insightful music teachers recognize that performance testing has been an integral part of measuring music achievement since instruments were first taught. The primary goal of learning a musical instrument is to perform, and this is emphasized in solo and ensemble performances at lessons, recitals, concerts, festivals, and competitions. Arrangements and compositions are two examples of student products. Performance testing, standardized tests, and teacher-constructed tests all have their purposes and should continue to be employed to assess music achievement. Techniques that might receive more attention are student self-assessment and peer assessment. As evidence of student-achievement growth over time, individual portfolios might be assembled to include video- and audiotaped performances, compositions, arrangements, written projects, and progress reports.

Measurement Tools

The most important measurement tools in instrumental music teaching are the teacher's and the students' ears. In addition to hearing music as it is performed, teachers and students must learn to analyze and critique constructively what is heard. It must not be assumed that students automatically determine their own weaknesses and strengths. Problems must be diagnosed and corrective techniques and materials prescribed. Ears must be trained to measure music achievement systematically. Ear training in instrumental music is dependent on development of audiation through a pattern vocabulary, a sense of tonality and meter, and models of sound. The previous chapters in this book have dealt with these topics in detail.

Instrumental performance achievement is measured through aural or visual observation techniques. Both should be as systematic and objective as possible. Aural observation—critical listening—of performance sounds may be done by teachers and students. In addition to listening for what is performed well, music teachers should listen to student performances with error detection and prescription in mind. Students may be taught to listen carefully to themselves and others and give constructive comments.

Visual observation of instrumental performance is used to assess what is physically being accomplished to produce the music. This is a primary measurement practice for instrumental technique objectives and is most effective when teachers and students observe themselves and each other and give constructive suggestions for improvement.

Rating Scales

Rating scales may be most familiar to instrumental teachers through their widespread use in solo and ensemble contests. Contest rating scales tend to center on evaluation rather than measurement and are more global in scope. Teachers may construct and use rating scales that are tailored to fit and measure specific performance objectives. Aural and visual observation of performance achievement can be improved and systematized objectively through use of rating scales. Rating scales may be constructed to fit any performance objective. Performance content that may be measured includes nearly all tonal and rhythm achievement along with most executive techniques. The data collected with teacher-made rating scales provide an ongoing record of individual student achievement and is an important aspect of curriculum evaluation.

The simplest form of rating scales is the checklist or additive scale. A checklist contains a series of statements that, when applied to performance, are determined by the rater as accomplished satisfactorily or unsatisfactorily. A point may be awarded for each task achieved. An example of such a checklist follows:

MINOR TONIC ARPEGGIOS CHECKLIST
(check each key when L D̄ M̄D̲ L̲ is performed accurately)

A minor	
D minor	E minor
G minor	B minor
C minor	F-sharp minor
F minor	C-sharp minor
B-flat minor	G-sharp minor
E-flat minor	D-sharp minor
A-flat minor	A-sharp minor

Because no continuum of content is necessary, the task may be attempted and completed in any order. Additive scales work best with discrete areas of performance knowledge such as scales, arpeggios, or chords in various keys and modes.

Another form of rating scale is constructed from five criteria statements in a continuum. The criteria are placed in sequential order from least to most difficult tasks, and more points are awarded as difficulty of task increases. For example:

INTONATION RATING SCALE

The overall intonation of the performance was

5—superior

4—excellent

3—average

2—fair

1—poor

This scale example allows for considerable subjectivity on the part of the rater because specific content is not attached to each criteria. This limits its usefulness as a measurement tool and is a common problem with contest rating scales of this type. Standards will vary among raters for any given performance, and individual raters may not be consistent among different performances over time. Note in the above rating scale that the highest number is assigned to the highest level (5 = superior). It is common to see this scale used in competitions with the number assignments reversed (1 = superior). This draws attention to analogous rankings in horse races and other sporting events where winning means being number one rather than using the scale as a measurement tool.

Rating scale subjectivity is minimized when the five criteria statements in the continuum are specific to content objectives. The performance task for the next rating scale example is for students to respond in tempo to a series of four recorded rhythm patterns. The same rating scale may be used with each task as students progress through the content and learning skills sequences. Content may be chosen with regard to learning skills sequence:

- echo-clapping patterns (A/O)
- echo-chanting patterns (VA)
- hearing the patterns sounded and chanting correct syllables (VA)
- echo-performing with an instrument while audiating syllables (VA)
- chanting syllables while reading the patterns (SA)
- performing the notated patterns with an instrument (SA)

Pattern content should fit whatever has been studied. The test patterns should be tape-recorded to eliminate performance errors and to guarantee that all students hear exactly the same patterns.

RHYTHM PATTERN RATING SCALE

5—no pattern errors

4—errors in one pattern

3—errors in two patterns

2—errors in three patterns

1—errors in four patterns

This rating scale allows the rater to be objective from student to student. Additional raters using the same scale with the same performance are likely to assign similar scores. The scale can easily be adapted for use with tonal patterns, again following the tasks within the learning skills sequence.

Many applications with varying content are possible with additive and continuous rating scales. The following six examples were presented by Saunders (1994) at a MENC convention session and represent some of the variety of possibilities. Saunders makes the point that these scales force the rater's attention to "what and how" the performance was rather than subjectively deciding how "good" it was.

INSTRUMENTAL PERFORMANCE RATING SCALE

Tonal Rating

The student performance of a prepared selection included

5) an accuracy of intonation throughout

4) nearly accurate intonation with a minimal amount of imprecise intervals

3) accurate intonation at the points of cadence (phrase endings); otherwise, there was a lack of precise intonation.

2) individual pitches included tonal center and the performance included an overall sense of tonality, however, with imprecise intervals and adjacent pitches

1) individual pitches that lacked tonal center and an overall sense of tonality

Rhythm Rating

The student instrumental performance of a prepared selection

5) was performed accurately with precise melodic rhythm

4) was performed nearly accurate, with a minimal amount of imprecise melodic rhythm

3) included a consistent tempo and recognizable meter throughout the performance, but also short continuous sections of imprecise melodic rhythms

2) included portions of consistent and inconsistent tempo and recognizable and unrecognizable meter with imprecise melodic rhythms

1) included a lack of consistent tempo and recognizable meter

Expression Rating
(additive)

The student instrumental performance of a prepared selection included appropriate

__overall tone quality

__style of articulation

__contrast of dynamics

__use of tempo rubato

__use of vibrato

INDIVIDUAL FLUTE PERFORMANCE RATING SCALE

Playing Position
(additive)

The student's holding and hand position included

__flute parallel to the lower lip

__flute blow hole centered on the lips

__fingers kept within 1/8–1/4 inch of the keys

__fingers centered on the keys

__arms slightly away from the body

Tone Quality

The student's tone

5) demonstrates a variety of tone colors

4) is centered throughout the lower octave

3) is centered throughout the middle and upper octaves

2) is focused, consisting of more tone than air

1) is airy, consisting of more air than tone

Vibrato

The student's sound

5) includes vibrato that varies with the style of the selection performed

4) has clearly audible wave intensity throughout the entire range

3) includes a diaphragmatic produced vibrato

2) includes vibrato

1) is straight, having no audible vibrato

Objectivity of rating scales may often be improved if they are used with tape-recorded performances rather than during the live performance. This eliminates distracting visual observations during test performances that may influence rater consistency. Students in class lessons and rehearsals may individually leave the room to tape-record a test performance in a separate recording location. The instructor may then listen to the tape at a later time and use appropriate rating scales to measure the performance.

Another recommended measurement technique for instrumental performance that uses rating scales is as follows: Three brief unfamiliar musical excerpts (approximately eight measures each) of teacher-composed material are selected. The excerpts are of the same difficulty level and are based on current achievement of the students to be tested. Excerpt 1 is given to students one week before the test date for home preparation without assistance. Excerpt 2 is given to students one week before the test date for preparation with teacher help. Excerpt 3 is sight-read during the testing period. All test performances are tape-recorded. The teacher then listens to the tapes and rates the performances using rating scales that reflect current teaching objectives and content. More than one rating scale may be applied to each performance, such as tonal patterns, consistent tempo, or tone quality. It is best to listen to the taped performances once for each rating scale used. The procedure takes minimal teacher time per student and results in useful measurement data. If used at the end of each grade period (six, nine, twelve, or eighteen weeks) during the school year, student performance progress is objectively documented.

Teacher-Made Tests

Many varieties of teacher-made tests may be used to measure instru-mental music achievement. Multiple choice, matching, and comple-tion tests are particularly appropriate forms for testing cognitive knowledge. Typical content would include: musical terms, composers, composition titles, historical information, key signatures, meter signa-tures, music theory, and instrument care. Written tests may be used on a regular basis to collect data related to content objectives.

A most useful type of teacher-made test is one in which items require students to respond to musical examples. Tape-recorded musi-cal examples may be constructed to test student musical perception and knowledge. Each item should include two to four response options. This type of item is especially useful for testing mode and meter recognition and for pattern vocabulary association with syllables and notation. Taped items may also be used to test student ability to echo patterns correctly with instruments and for pattern and melodic dictation tests.

A few examples of multiple-choice, matching, true-false, and com-pletion items are included here. The reader should consult a textbook, such as those listed at the end of this chapter, for detailed instruction in item writing.

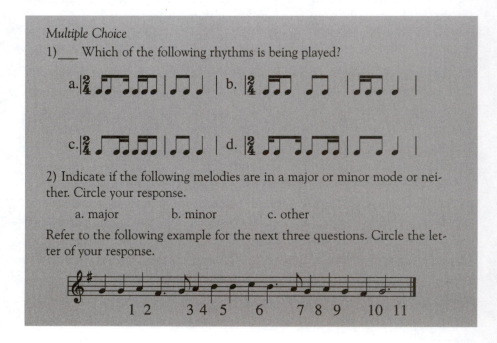

Multiple Choice

1)___ Which of the following rhythms is being played?

2) Indicate if the following melodies are in a major or minor mode or nei-ther. Circle your response.

    a. major   b. minor   c. other

Refer to the following example for the next three questions. Circle the let-ter of your response.

3) In this example, a measure line should occur at which of the following numbers?

a. 1, 3, 7, 9, 11   c. 2, 5, 8, 10, 11

b. 1, 4, 8, 10, 11   d. 2, 4, 6, 8, 10, 11

4) The interval between the fourth and the fifth note is __?__.

a. a half step   c. a step and a half

b. a whole step   d. a minor third

5) The name of the tune in the above example is

a. "Over the River"   c. "Sweet Betsy from Pike"

b. "America"   d. "The Star-Spangled Banner"

Matching

6) Draw a line from the meter signature to the rhythm patterns that would complete one tempo beat in duration.

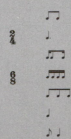

True-False

Circle the correct answer.

7) True   False   Cut time (alla breve) is indicated by $\frac{2}{4}$

8) True   False   A flat lowers a pitch by a whole step.

Completion

9) Locate *do* with a whole note on the staff.

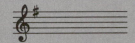 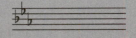 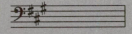

10) Use music notation to write the rhythms you hear.

2   6   2
4   8   4

In Item 1, it is best to use a prerecorded set of rhythm patterns that has been carefully produced. Each response has the same number of sounds, to avert possible answering by counting only sounds. The sound source may be a wind, string, percussion, or keyboard instrument. Chanted patterns may be used for easier items. Use four possible responses whenever possible in multiple choice formats.

Item 2 should also use prerecorded brief excerpts that are clearly in major, minor, or another mode. Possible examples are melodies with or without accompaniment, keyboard selections, or ensemble music. Excerpts from familiar selections should be easier than from unfamiliar music.

Items 3–5 are examples for students to apply music knowledge and audiation skills to a segment of music notation in order to determine answers.

Item 6 is a matching item that is a special kind of multiple-choice response. It is best to restrict matching items to one concept each; in this example, recognizing familiar tempo beat patterns in duple and triple.

Items 7–8 are propositions that are stated as plausible but are actually false. True items are usually easier to write.

Item 9 tests finding *do* given a key signature. Use appropriate clefs.

Item 10 is rhythm dictation. Use two or four tempo beats of patterns and repeat them once. Again, it is best to use prerecorded sound sources that are accurately produced. Items are easier if syllables are also chanted.

Portfolio Assessment

A basic measurement technique for authentic assessment is portfolio development. Student portfolios are collections of materials over time that may be viewed as evidence of achievement, breadth of learning, and overall progress. The learning process is emphasized as much or more than the product. As a result, it is primarily a qualitative rather than quantitative process. Davidson, et al. (1992) from Harvard University's Project Zero, along with the Educational Testing Service has developed an experimental program in the arts known as Arts PROPEL in the Pittsburgh, Pennsylvania, schools. They advocate portfolio assessment that includes examples of student's perception, reflection, and production in the arts, including music. Of these three aspects, student reflection as part of the learning process is probably least used in traditional measurement of music instruction. Reflection includes students critiquing themselves and others in order to develop critical thinking skills and self-assessment of their musical achievement. A portfolio of an instrumental music student might include audio- and videotapes of individual performances throughout the school year; written critiques of individual and ensemble playing; journals with entries about how and what they are learning; and written assignments and tests. Portfolios may be examined by teachers, students, and parents at the ends of grading periods and recommendations made.

Portfolio assessment is a time-consuming process, with problems in reliably measuring student progress, objectively interpreting the product, and determining grades. It may be difficult to implement by instrumental teachers with large numbers of students. One of its main advantages is the regular and direct involvement of students in the assessment and critiquing process. This can be an important motivation and learning factor for students.

Technology

Technology has evolved that integrates personal computers with audio and visual equipment, and this holds special promise for applications in music measurement and evaluation. Computer software is very useful for keeping records of achievement data from large numbers of students. Records may be stored of data in forms including numbers, words, music notation, pictures, and musical sounds. Computer assisted instructional programs often include scoring and record keeping features. As the technology proliferates and more applications are designed and implemented, school instrumental music programs will benefit from increased possibilities for meaningful measurement.

Measuring Objectives

The final sections of Chapters 3 and 4 contain lists of objectives for tonal and rhythm content. The content sequence of the lists of objectives is repeated below as examples for applying measurement techniques.

Tonal and rhythm content within objectives may be changed as needed to fit the tonal or rhythm content sequences described in Chapters
3 and 4; major and minor could be changed to dorian and mixolydian,
for example, or duple and triple could be changed to unusual meter;
tonic could be changed to dominant-seventh; tempo and meter beat
patterns could be changed to subdivision or elongation patterns, and
so on. Combining different content lists of objectives through overlapping as indicated in Chapters 3 and 4 is not included. Both content
and learning sequences are incorporated in the tonal and rhythm lists.
In addition, lists of objectives for technical skills of instrument families
are included.

A measurement technique (labeled MT) follows each of the objective statements listed here. Each measurement technique is a sugges-
tion pertaining to collection of data relative to student achievement
for that particular objective. Many other techniques may also be
employed. Teachers may use measurement techniques in formal testing situations where collected data is recorded or in informal achievement assessment during the course of instruction.

Tonal Objectives and Measurement Techniques

The student will be able to

1. sing/play familiar major and minor songs without notation
    (A/O).
MT: Teacher aurally assesses individual performances of assigned
    songs performed without notation. Rating scales may be used.
2. sing/play major and minor tonic arpeggios with syllables but
    without notation (VA).
MT: Teacher assesses recorded individual performances of assigned
    tonic arpeggios with appropriate rating scale.
3. recognize aurally major and minor resting tones (A/O).
MT: Students listen to taped test items of short unfamiliar songs
    with three ending choices and choose which response ends on
    the resting tone.
4. label familiar songs as major or minor mode after hearing or
    performing without notation (VA).
MT: Students listen to and identify taped test items of phrases from

familiar songs using an answer sheet with three response
choices—major, minor, other—for each item.

5. label unfamiliar songs as major or minor mode after hearing
without notation (G).

MT: Students listen to and identify taped test items of phrases from
unfamiliar songs using an answer sheet with three response
choices—major, minor, other—for each item.

6. echo-sing/-play major and minor tonic function tonal patterns
without syllables or notation (A/O).

MT: Teacher listens to individuals echo-sing/-play ten patterns each
and records number of the patterns echoed accurately.

7. echo-sing major and minor tonic function tonal patterns with
tonal syllables and without notation (VA).

MT: Teacher listens to individuals echo-sing ten patterns each and
records number of patterns echoed with correct tonal syllables
and accurate intonation.

8. sing major and minor tonic function tonal patterns with tonal
syllables after hearing patterns performed without notation
(VA).

MT: Teacher plays patterns and records number of patterns sung
accurately with syllables.

9. recognize aurally major and minor tonic function tonal patterns in familiar songs without notation (PS). (At this point,
overlap objectives by simultaneously beginning a content
sequence at number 6 with major and minor dominant-seventh
function tonal patterns.)

MT: Teacher asks students to audiate a familiar song and to write
which words in the song correspond to previously specified patterns, such as S $\underline{D}$ $\overline{M}$.

10. recognize aurally major and minor tonic function tonal patterns in unfamiliar songs without notation (G).

MT: Teacher performs an unfamiliar song and student raises hand
whenever previously specified pattern, such as D $\overline{M}$ $\overline{S}$, occurs.

11. sing and play self-created combinations of familiar major and
minor tonic function tonal patterns without notation (C/I).
(At this point, overlap objectives by simultaneously beginning
a content sequence at number 6 with major and minor subdominant function tonal patterns.)

MT: Teacher rates accuracy of student assignment to choose any six familiar tonal patterns, combine them without notation, sing them with syllables, and then perform them.

12. recognize familiar major and minor tonic function tonal patterns in notation (SA).

MT: Teacher performs selected familiar patterns from ten tonal pattern flash cards, and students respond by indicating which flash card was performed.

13. sing with syllables, write, and play notated major and minor tonic function tonal patterns (SA). (At this point, overlap objectives by simultaneously beginning a content sequence at number 6 with supertonic, submediant, mediant function and chromatic tonal patterns.)

MT: a) Teacher provides notation of familiar patterns on flash cards and records accuracy of student responses of singing with tonal syllables or performing on instruments; b) teacher performs familiar patterns for students to write with correct notation.

14. recognize and sing/play familiar major and minor tonic function tonal patterns within notation of familiar songs (CS).

MT: Teacher performs selected familiar patterns from a specific song. While observing the notation for the song, students respond by circling the performed patterns.

15. recognize and sing/play familiar major and minor tonic function tonal patterns within notation of unfamiliar songs (G).

MT: a) Teacher performs selected familiar patterns from an unfamiliar song. While observing the notation for an unfamiliar song, students respond by circling the performed patterns; b) While observing the notation for an unfamiliar song, students are tested by how many familiar tonal patterns they can recognize and perform.

16. improvise, compose, and perform combinations of familiar written major and minor tonic function tonal patterns (C/I).

MT: a) Teacher rates student-improvised variations of familiar written songs; b) teacher rates student-written composition assignments; c) teacher rates student performances of compositions.

17. understand the theoretical basis for harmonic function of major and minor tonic function tonal patterns (TU).

MT: Students take a written test on knowledge of scale and chord writing.

Rhythm Objectives and Measurement Techniques

The student will be able to

1. respond to the sound of music with consistent tempo-beat movements (A/O).

MT: Teacher observes student accuracy in responding to tempo beats with patting movements while listening to songs and rates accuracy.

2. respond to the sound of duple meter music with consistent pat-clapping movements (A/O).

MT: Teacher observes and rates student accuracy in responding to duple meter songs with pat-clapping on meter beats.

3. respond to the sound of triple meter music with consistent pat-clap-clapping movements (A/O).

MT: Teacher observes and rates student accuracy in responding to triple meter songs with pat-clap-clapping on meter beats.

4. recognize aurally familiar music without notation as duple or triple meter feeling (A/O).

MT: Teacher provides taped excerpts of familiar songs in duple or triple meter feelings. Students decide whether or not the songs fit the pat-clap or pat-clap-clap movements and circle *p-c*, *p-c-c*, or other for each item on an answer sheet.

5. label familiar music as duple or triple meter feeling without notation (VA).

MT: Students listen to taped test items of phrases from familiar songs in duple, triple, and unusual meters and choose meter type and label from three response options—duple, triple, other—on an answer sheet.

6. label unfamiliar music as duple or triple meter feeling without notation (G).

MT: Students listen to taped test items of phrases from unfamiliar songs in duple, triple, and unusual meters and choose meter type and label from three response options—duple, triple, other—on an answer sheet.

7. echo-clap/-play duple and triple meter melodic rhythm patterns without notation that coincide with underlying tempo and meter beats (A/O).

MT: Teacher listens to individuals echo-clap/-play ten patterns each and records number of patterns echoed accurately.

8. echo-chant duple and triple tempo- and meter-beat patterns with rhythm syllables and without notation (VA).

MT: Teacher listens to individuals echo-chant ten patterns each and records number of patterns echoed with correct rhythm syllables and consistent meter feeling.

9. chant syllables for duple and triple tempo- and meter-beat patterns after hearing patterns sounded without notation (VA).

MT: Teacher claps patterns and records number of patterns chanted accurately with syllables.

10. recognize aurally duple and triple tempo and meter beat patterns in familiar songs without notation (PS). (At this point, overlap objectives by simultaneously beginning a content sequence at number 7 with duple and triple meter patterns that elongate underlying tempo and meter beats or that subdivide meter beats.)

MT: Teacher asks students to audiate a familiar song and then write which words in the song correspond to previously specified patterns, such as 1 ta ne ta.

11. recognize aurally duple and triple tempo and meter beat patterns in unfamiliar songs without notation (G).

MT: Teacher performs an unfamiliar song and student raises hand whenever a previously specified pattern, such as 1 ne ta, occurs.

12. clap/chant/play self-created combinations of familiar duple and triple tempo- and meter-beat patterns without notation (C/I). (At this point, overlap objectives by simultaneously beginning a content sequence at number 7 with unusual meter melodic rhythm patterns that coincide with underlying tempo and meter beats.)

MT: Teacher rates accuracy of student assignment to choose any six familiar rhythm patterns, combine them without notation, chant them with syllables, and perform them.

13. recognize duple and triple tempo- and meter-beat patterns from notation (SA).

MT: Teacher performs selected familiar patterns from ten rhythm pattern flash cards. Students respond by indicating which pattern was performed.

14. clap/chant/play duple and triple tempo- and meter-beat patterns from notation (SA).

MT: Teacher provides notation of familiar patterns on flash cards and records accuracy of student responses of clapping, chanting, and/or playing.

15. recognize, clap/chant/play familiar duple and triple tempo and meter beat patterns within notation of familiar songs (CS).

MT: Teacher performs selected familiar patterns from a specific song. While observing the notation for the song, students respond by circling the performed patterns.

16. recognize, clap/chant/play familiar duple and triple tempo- and meter-beat patterns within notation of unfamiliar songs (G). (At this point, overlap objectives by simultaneously beginning a content sequence at number 7 with unusual meter patterns that elongate underlying tempo and meter beats or subdivide meter beats.)

MT: Teacher performs selected familiar patterns from an unfamiliar song. While observing the notation for the unfamiliar song, students respond by circling the performed patterns.

17. improvise, compose, and perform combinations of familiar written duple and triple tempo- and meter-beat patterns (C/I).

MT: a) Teacher rates student-improvised rhythmic variations of a familiar written song; b) teacher rates student-written composition assignments; c) teacher rates students' performances of compositions.

18. understand the theoretical basis for metric function of duple and triple tempo- and meter-beat patterns (TU).

MT: Student takes written test on knowledge of meter signatures and note value proportionalities.

Instrument Techniques Objectives

The technical aspects of playing an instrument are directly related to the demands of the musical objectives. Instrument technique results from studying and performing music. Learning technique outside a musical context is a questionable practice. The objectives in the following lists have no particular sequence for learning but are, for the most part, all in effect from the first lesson and continue throughout instruction. The specifics for each objective depend on the musical demands.

Accomplishment of instrument techniques is measured primarily through direct visual and aural observations by the teacher, student, or other students. The content of most technique objectives does not lend itself well to continuum ratings. The decision to be made in most cases is satisfactory or unsatisfactory performance. For this reason, the lists below do not include a measurement technique for each objective. The measurement technique for all objectives is the same: The teacher observes and rates instrument technique performance as satisfactory or unsatisfactory.

Technique Objectives for All Instruments

Students will be able to perform

1. with correct finger and hand positions
2. with acceptable body posture
3. with acceptable and characteristic tone quality
4. with acceptable intonation
5. effective tuning procedures for the instrument

Technique Objectives for Wind Instruments

Students will be able to perform

1. correct assembly procedures for the instrument
2. with correct holding and support of the instrument
3. with correct embouchure formation
4. with effective breath support
5. tongue movements for various articulations (e.g., legato, marcato, staccato)
6. with controlled and accurate finger technique
7. with controlled and pleasing vibrato

Technique Objectives for Stringed Instruments

Students will be able to perform

1. with correct right-hand position for holding the bow

2. with correct left-hand position and support of the instrument
3. various bowing articulations (e.g., legato, marcato, staccato)
4. pizzicato technique
5. with controlled and accurate left-hand fingering technique
6. various left-hand techniques (e.g., shifting, double stops, vibrato)

Technique Objectives for Percussion Instruments

Students will be able to perform

1. with appropriate instrument heights and positions
2. with correct stick and mallet handholds
3. on appropriate striking locations of instruments
4. with controlled stick technique (e.g., single taps, double bounce, multiple bounce)
5. with controlled mallet technique
6. with various articulation effects

Using Standardized Music Tests

Published standardized tests of music achievement and aptitude are important measurement tools for teaching instrumentalists. Unlike teacher-made tests and rating scales, published tests include established norm tables and are standardized with regard to administration and scoring. They afford the advantages of high-quality, well-constructed test materials and comparisons of students' scores with norm groups. Most tests have machine-scorable answer sheets that may be scored by hand or by computer optical scanning. Most tests can be administered to groups of students. The best source of information about a test is the test manual, which should include extensive explanation of the test content, administration, scoring procedures, norm groups, test reliability, test validity, and score interpretation.

During the past seventy-five years, a number of music achievement tests have been published in this country, most of them designed for school use. The most important consideration when choosing a published achievement test is whether the test content fits your content objectives. The content and format of published achievement tests become dated with time, so avoid older tests, which have gone out of print. Achievement tests are most useful to measure long-term objectives, usually once or twice per school year. Score comparisons to national norms may be made; equally important, local norms may be established over years of repeated testing. It is generally inappropriate to use scores obtained from published tests for determining music grades.

A number of music aptitude tests have been published since the turn of the century in this country. Aptitude testing has undergone many changes as testing technology and the understanding of aptitude have evolved. Music aptitude may be defined as the potential to achieve musically. Many variables constitute music aptitude, but there is considerable research evidence that three of the main components are tonal, rhythm, and musical sensitivity. Music-aptitude tests should not require previous formal music training in order to take the tests. Some tests published as aptitude tests are mainly achievement tests because the student must have musical training in order to answer the test items.

Aptitude testing is especially appropriate before beginning students on instruments. A reliable and valid aptitude test aids in identifying students who may achieve musically, and in diagnosing musical strengths and weaknesses. Teaching efficiency and student success are directly affected. Aptitude tests should never be used as selection tools to decide who may or may not receive instrumental instruction.

At least four common misconceptions exist about music aptitude testing and its relationship to beginning instrumentalists. The first is that student interest in starting instrumental instruction is a measure of aptitude. Research by Gordon (1967) and others has shown that little or no relationship exists between interest and aptitude. Although interest may be a deciding factor to begin instrumental instruction, it never substitutes for the music aptitude necessary for long-term commitment and success with an instrument. The second misconception is that academic aptitude (usually represented with IQ scores) is a measure of music aptitude. Again, there is considerable research evidence—for example, Young's (1971) study—that IQ test scores have only a slight relationship to music aptitude. In short, IQ scores should never be used to select students for instrumental study. High to low music aptitude can be found in groups of individuals with high IQ scores, in groups with low IQ scores, or in groups with average IQs.

The third misconception about music aptitude testing is that the promotional materials distributed by instrument companies are aptitude tests. Although many are labeled as such, none of these materials has proven reliability or validity as aptitude tests. At best, they may be used to generate interest, but they are frequently misused in schools by well-intentioned instructors. The fourth and last point of error is that aptitude tests may be teacher-constructed. This is analogous to teachers developing IQ tests in their schools. The complexity of a psychometrically sound aptitude test is beyond the scope of teacher construction; teacher-made achievement tests, however, are appropriate.

Selected published music achievement and aptitude tests are described here on the basis of content, quality of the test construction, and appropriateness for use with instrumental students. It must be emphasized that no test has value if the teacher does not understand how to interpret the scores. Measurement texts such as those by Thorndike and Hagen (1977) or Ebel and Frisbie (1991) should prove most helpful.

Published Music Achievement Tests

Iowa Tests of Music Literacy (ITML), revised, by Edwin Gordon (1991), published by GIA Publications, Inc., 7404 South Mason Avenue, Chicago, IL 60638; first published (1970) by the Bureau of Educational Research and Service, University of Iowa.

ITML is a tape-recorded test in six levels of difficulty. Each level contains two main tests, Tonal Audiation and Rhythm Audiation. Each main test contains three subtests: Aural Perception (e.g., Is what you hear major or minor, duple or triple?), Reading Recognition (Is what you see what you hear?), and Notational Understanding (Complete the notation to fit what you hear). Each level takes about ninety minutes to administer, but any of the six subtests may be given on separate occasions. The item content is originally composed melodic and rhythmic fragments performed on a synthesizer. The manual contains percentile norm tables for levels 1–3 in grades 4–6, 7–9, and 10–12; and for levels 4–6 in grades 7–9 and 10–12. Answer sheets may be hand or machine scored.

ITML is appropriate for beginning through advanced instrumental students. A profile of tonal and rhythm achievement progress may be charted if appropriate levels of the test are administered once or twice per school year. Because of the unfamiliar tonal and rhythm pattern content of the items and the norm tables based on a national sample, these tests are particularly appropriate for summative measurement of instrumentalists.

Music Achievement Tests 1–4 (MAT) by Richard Colwell (1968, 1969, 1970), published by MAT, Inc., 84 Fuller Street #1, Brookline, MA 02146.

MAT is a set of four tests, each available on a long-playing record. The content is related to general music basal series of the 1960s. The test content is not sequenced by difficulty levels and need not be administered in chronological order. Each test contains three or four separate parts: Test 1—Pitch Discrimination, Interval Discrimination, Meter Discrimination; Test 2—Major-Minor Mode Discrimination, Feeling for Tonal Center, Auditory-Visual Discrimination; Test 3— Tonal Memory, Melody Recognition, Pitch Recognition, Instrument Recognition; Test 4—Musical Style, Auditory-Visual Discrimination, Chord Recognition, Cadence Recognition. Item content, for the most part, consists of excerpts from familiar tunes. Percentile and standard score norm tables are furnished for Test 1 and Test 2 for individual grades 4–8 and for high school students. Norms for Test 3 and Test 4 are available individually for grades 4–12. In addition, combined norms are included for grades 4–6, 7–9, and 10–12 for students with instrumental experience. Answer sheets may be hand or machine scored. Many of the individual subtests may be used with instrumental students whenever content objectives coincide.

The Watkins-Farnum Performance Scale (WFPS), Forms A and B, by John Watkins and Stephen Farnum (1954), published by Hal Leonard Music, Inc., Winona, MN; and the Farnum String Scale by Stephen Farnum (1969), published by Hal Leonard Music, Inc.

The WFPS and its later variation, the Farnum String Scale, are the only published attempts at performance testing of solo instruments. Two equivalent forms of the test are available. The WFPS consists of fourteen études that are claimed to be of increasing difficulty. The same études are performed individually by all instruments except snare drum. While a student sight-reads the études, the rater records errors of pitch, rhythm (incorrect durations, rests, holds, and pauses), tempo changes, expression, slurs, and repeats. Any one error per measure of notation results in the loss of a point, and scoring does not distinguish among types of errors. The manual includes limited reliability and validity information. Reported norms are inadequate.

The WFPS is most usable as a performance rating when norms are developed locally for each instrument. It is not advisable to compare scores among different instruments or to use the results to award music grades. Possible uses of the test include using scores to determine seating challenges and as sight-reading scores at ends of semesters.

Published Music Aptitude Tests

Musical Aptitude Profile (MAP) by Edwin Gordon, published by the Riverside Publishing Company, Chicago (1988); first published by Houghton Mifflin (1965).

MAP is a tape-recorded aptitude test with three main sections, each with subtests: Tonal Imagery—Melody, Harmony; Rhythm Imagery—Tempo, Meter; Musical Sensitivity—Phrasing, Balance, and Style. The test is designed for group administration to students in grades 4–12. Three fifty-minute periods are recommended to complete administration. No formal music achievement is required to take the test. Students need take the test only once in their school careers. The test manual includes directions for administering, scoring, and interpreting results. Separate norm tables are included for grades 4–12. Answer sheets may be hand or machine scored. MAP is the only music-aptitude test developed to this date that has established predictive validity for instrumental music success (Gordon, 1967; Froseth, 1971).

Intermediate Measures of Music Audiation (IMMA) by Edwin Gordon, published by GIA Publications, Inc., Chicago (1982).

IMMA is a tape-recorded aptitude test in two parts, Tonal and Rhythm. The test is designed for repeated group testing of students in grades 1–4. About forty minutes is needed to administer the test. No formal music training is needed to take the test. Item content consists of pairs of tonal and rhythm patterns that students are to determine as same or different. The manual contains information for administering, scoring, and interpreting the test. Percentile norms are included for each grade. Answer sheets must be hand scored. IMMA should be of particular interest to teachers of keyboard and stringed instruments for use with students between six and nine years of age.

Advanced Measures of Music Audiation (AMMA) by Edwin Gordon, published by GIA Publications, Inc., Chicago (1989).

AMMA is a tape-recorded test that requires about sixteen minutes of listening to thirty pairs of musical statements and answers sounded by a synthesizer. The testing task is to determine if the answers are the same as the statements; or, if different, whether the difference is a tonal or rhythm change. Answer sheets are hand scored and provide tonal, rhythm, and composite test scores. A brief test manual includes norm tables for college music majors, non-music majors, and high school students. Although the test was developed primarily for use with entering college students, it is also usable with upper-level high school students as an indicator of music aptitude levels.

Recording Achievement Data

If musical and instrument technique objectives are systematically taught and measured, productive evaluation is possible. An interim step between measurement and evaluation processes is recording and transforming the data into meaningful information. Scores from aural and visual observations in the forms of teacher-made tests or rating scales provide quantified evidence for use in achievement evaluation. The raw scores from the variety of achievement measurements should be carefully collected for each student. Record books may be purchased or each student may be assigned a page in a three-ring binder for entering achievement information. Spreadsheet software and personal computers are widely available and an excellent means to facilitate both data storage and computation. Data must be regularly recorded after being collected. These data may then be interpreted and used to assess progress and to assign grades.

Music teachers sometimes feel that achievement-data collection and recording process is overwhelming because of the large numbers of students involved in their programs. A solution may be to have students manage most of the record keeping. An example of this is explained in a study by Zurcher (1987) in which he compared three procedures for keeping records of achievement of eighth-grade band students. He employed a point system and compared the effects of students keeping their own records, the teacher giving assigned daily grades along with feedback, and the teacher giving grades with no feedback until the end of the grading period. Students accumulated points for various tasks and achievements and were provided with options to redeem the points for various rewards. The student record-keeping process was more accurate and successful in promoting higher achievement than were the other two procedures.

Transforming, Combining, and Weighting Scores

One of the purposes of measuring music achievement is to obtain objective data in numerical form. Quantified information may be accumulated and appropriately interpreted over periods of time. Raw score achievement information for each student is typically summarized and interpreted at the end of grading periods. Checklist data of satisfactory or unsatisfactory achievement for stated objectives are easily interpreted. Certain precautions must be observed when combining raw score data from tests and rating scales in order for the final results to be meaningful and fair for each student.

Raw scores are uninterpretable unless they undergo transformations that allow comparisons and combinations. Some of the most common score transformations are as follows:

1. Scores are sometimes rank-ordered from highest to lowest and the distribution is arbitrarily divided into segments that are assigned letter grades. This procedure introduces subjectivity and loss of precision in the data.

2. Scores may be converted to percentages of correct items on a given test. The percentages may then be converted to predetermined categories of letter grades. Each student is in effect measured against the predetermined percentage amount of test content answered correctly. Percentage scores do not refer to any ranking or normative comparisons of students. If a predetermined grade scale is used (e.g., 94–100 percent = A, 88–93 percent = B, and so forth), students automatically know their grades when they receive their percentage score. Although this procedure is relatively easy to accomplish, the validity of the grade is based on the assumption that the test items are truly representative of the domain of knowledge being tested, and that the test is highly reliable, which in practice is seldom realized. For example, the real question becomes not one of student achievement but whether or not 80 percent of one particular test accurately represents grade C, or "average" work.

3. Another transformation is to rank-order scores from highest to lowest and then to convert them to percentiles. A given percentile defines the percentage of individuals who took the test and scored at or below the particular score associated with the percentile. Receiving a score at the fifty-fifth percentile means that 55 percent of the students taking the test scored at or below that particular score. This is a normative transformation that compares each student to all others in the testing group. Ideally, the size of the group should be relatively large (over fifty) for this transformation to function well. Letter grades may be arbitrarily assigned to percentile groups after the tests are scored so students will not know their grades when given their percentile ranks only.

4. Standard score transformations are the only type that retain the absolute differences between raw scores. Standard scores can be directly combined and proportionately weighted. Because they relate to the properties of the normal distribution curve, standard scores are inappropriate when used with highly skewed distributions and with small groups (less than thirty). There are a number of standard score transformations possible; one of the most useful for test data is the T-score transformation. T-scores convert a distribution of raw scores to a mean of fifty and a standard deviation of ten. T-scores are obtained by first calculating the mean and standard deviation for the score distribution. A raw score is then transformed to a T-score by (a) subtracting

the mean and dividing by the standard deviation, and (b) multiplying by ten and adding fifty. T-scores from different tests and ratings may be directly combined or proportionally weighted to obtain summary data for determining achievement levels and grades.

Remember, it is not appropriate simply to add a student's raw scores together from different tests and ratings. This inadvertently gives different weightings to specific scores unless the standard deviations for each test distribution are similar in size. It is beyond the scope of this chapter to elaborate further on correct procedures for transforming, combining, and weighting raw-score achievement data; the reader should consult the measurement texts listed at the close of the chapter for additional information.

Reporting Instrumental Music Achievement

Results and interpretations of measurement data from instrumental music achievement need regular reporting procedures. It is important to report achievement results to students, parents, and administrators so that the extent to which objectives are met is obvious to all concerned. Students gain perspective of their achievement level. Parents become more aware of content objectives through the reporting procedures. Administrators are able to assess program strengths and weaknesses through accurately reported data.

Many instrumental instructors are uncertain about exactly what or how to report evaluations. Marks should clearly reflect achievement levels defined by specific musical and instrument technique objectives. Achievement marks are not interpretable if such other information as attendance, attitude, and effort are mixed with achievement data. Report cards may include separate areas for attendance and subjective evaluations of classroom behavior and effort. Record keeping is then simplified, and all data are easily interpreted and understood.

It is advisable to use a separate written form to report instrumental achievement in addition to the usual academic report card. The instrumental report card or progress report may then be tailored to the needs of the particular school system and program. Individual reports of instrumental achievement should be specific enough to reflect current levels of attainment accurately but should not be so detailed that they are cumbersome for the instructor to complete.

A format for an instrumental music progress report is displayed in Figure 7.1. Specific tonal, rhythmic, and technical objectives taken from the lists earlier in this chapter would be included as needed in each section. Numbers of students in the class totals who received O, S, U, or N are reported to allow meaningful comparisons. The report is designed for four grade periods of nine weeks each in a typical school year. Students receive an O, S, U, or N for each objective that would be listed in the appropriate sections of the report. No overall grade is given. Fewer or more grading periods could be used. This progress report format and letter grades is designed for elementary or middle school instrumental content. It may be adapted for high school students by adjusting the content objectives and letter designations as needed.

Variations to consider with the format in Figure 7.1 are as follows:

1. Different letter designations may be used. Regardless of the number of letter marks used or what letters are chosen, it is essential that clear definitions of each category are listed on the report.
2. Specific lists of technique objectives for woodwinds, brass, percussion, and strings may be included with the appropriate section used for each student.
3. A separate section for behavior and attitude assessment may be added.
4. A separate section may be added to report Musical Aptitude Profile percentile rankings.
5. The back of the report or a separate sheet may be used to explain content objectives further to parents.
6. A separate section may be added to list objectives for music knowledge—terms, composers, forms, etc.
7. Effort may be reported for each objective by adding another column of boxes for grade periods and using the same letter designations.
8. Blank space for written comments by the instructor or by parents may be added.

An example of a progress report that includes many of the options mentioned above appears in Figure 7.2. The content may be placed on

Name_____Grade Level_____

O = Outstanding   S = Satisfactory progress   U = Unsatisfactory progress
N = Not measured this grade period

Grade Period

	1	2	3	4
Class Totals O				
S				
U				

Days Absent

1 2 3 4		Tonal Objectives
| | | | |	1.	
	2.	
	3.	
	.	

1 2 3 4		Rhythm Objectives
| | | | |	1.	
	2.	
	3.	
	.	

1 2 3 4		Technique Objectives
| | | | |	1.	
	2.	
	3.	
	.	

Parent Signature   1._____
                        2._____
                        3._____
                        4._____

Figure 7.1   FORMAT FOR AN INSTRUMENTAL MUSIC
PROGRESS REPORT

Name_____Grade___ Instrument_____

O = Outstanding S= Satisfactory I = Improving
U = Unsatisfactory N = Not Applicable

RHYTHM SKILLS

_____Demonstrates accurate movements to tempo and meter beats

_____Recognizes duple and triple meters (without/with notation)

_____Uses rhythm syllables accurately (without/with notation)

_____Reads and performs rhythm notation accurately

TONAL SKILLS

_____Sings tonal patterns accurately

_____Recognizes major and minor (without/with notation)

_____Uses tonal syllables accurately (without/with notation)

_____Reads and performs tonal notation accurately

TECHNIQUE SKILLS—BRASS AND WOODWIND

_____Hand position: Holds instrument with correct hand positions

_____Fingerings/slide positions: Demonstrates correct fingerings and slide positions

_____Embouchure: Demonstrates correct lip formation for producing a good sound

_____Breath control: Is progressing in ability to sustain a tone or phrase

_____Articulation: Accurately performs tongue and slur markings

_____Range: Is progressing in ability to extend playing range

_____Tuning: Can adjust tones to correct pitches

Figure 7.2 EXAMPLE OF INSTRUMENTAL MUSIC
PROGRESS REPORT

the front and back of a sheet and completed at least two or preferably four times in a school year for each student. The Rhythm Skills, Tonal Skills, Other, and Responsibility sections are completed for all students, and the appropriate Technique Skills section is chosen according to the instrument.

TECHNIQUE SKILLS: PERCUSSION

_____Hand position: Holds sticks and mallets with correct hand positions

_____Wrist action: Performs with correct, flexible wrist motions

_____Sticking: Accurately performs the stick markings in the music

_____Rolls: Is improving in ability to control bounces and accurately performs roll drills

_____Rudiments: Is improving in ability to perform standard rudiments (rolls, flams, paradiddles, etc.)

TECHNIQUE SKILLS: STRINGS

_____Draws bow in straight line in correct placement on strings

_____Performs bow markings accurately as indicated in music

_____Draws bow with a relaxed wrist

_____Demonstrates knowledge of pitches at different locations (positions) on the fingerboard

_____Demonstrates progress in left hand shifting positions while playing

_____Demonstrates progress in using vibrato appropriately

_____Tuning: Can adjust tones to correct pitches

OTHER

_____Transposes songs and patterns by ear

_____Improvises with familiar tonal and rhythm patterns

_____Composes simple melodies using familiar patterns

RESPONSIBILITY

_____Demonstrates adequate preparation of assignments by regular home practice

_____Demonstrates proper care of instrument

_____Remembers to bring music and instrument to lessons and rehearsals

Figure 7.2 (CONTINUED)   EXAMPLE OF INSTRUMENTAL MUSIC PROGRESS REPORT

Review Questions

1. What is the basis for evaluation of instrumental music achievement?
2. Why should regular measurement of objectives occur?

3. Why is it important to measure music achievement of individual students?
4. What place does visual observation have as a measurement tool?
5. How may subjectivity be controlled when constructing and using rating scales?
6. Discuss how portfolio assessment might be incorporated into instrumental music programs.
7. How might you measure students' ability to recognize minor tonic and dominant function tonal patterns in notation?
8. How might you measure students' ability to perform self-created combinations of familiar triple meter patterns?
9. How might you measure students' ability to form a correct embouchure?
10. What advantages do published standardized tests have over teacher-made tests?
11. For what purposes should music-aptitude tests be administered?
12. How do achievement tests differ from aptitude tests?
13. What measurement data should be reported to students, and why should it be reported?

References

DAVIDSON, LYLE, et al. (1992). *ARTS PROPEL: A handbook for music*. Princeton: Educational Testing Service and Harvard Project Zero.

EBEL, ROBERT L., and DAVID A. FRISBIE. (1991). *Essentials of educational measurement*, 5th ed. Englewood Cliffs, NJ: Prentice-Hall, Inc.

FROSETH, JAMES O. (1971). Using MAP scores in the instruction of beginning students in instrumental music. *Journal of Research in Music Education* 19 (1), 98–105.

GORDON, EDWIN E. (1967). *A three-year longitudinal predictive validity study of the Musical Aptitude Profile*. Iowa City: University of Iowa Press.

SAUNDERS, T. CLARK. (1994). The assessment of music skill learning: Techniques for the classroom and rehearsal. Session handout from the MENC In-Service Conference, Cincinnati, Ohio.

THORNDIKE, ROBERT L., and ELIZABETH HAGEN. (1977). *Measurement and evaluation in psychology and education*, 4th ed. New York: John Wiley and Sons.

YOUNG, WILLIAM T. (1971). The role of musical aptitude, intelligence, and academic achievement in predicting the musical attainment of elementary instrumental students. *Journal of Research in Music Education* 19 (4), 385–398.

ZURCHER, WILLIAM. (1987). The effect of three evaluation procedures on the rehearsal achievement of eighth-grade band students. In *Applications of research in music behavior*, eds. Clifford K. Madsen and Carol A. Prickett. Tuscaloosa, AL: University of Alabama Press, 51–58.

For Further Reading

BOYLE, J. DAVID, and RUDOLF E.RADOCY. (1987). *Measurement and evaluation of musical experiences*. New York: Schirmer Books..

GORDON, EDWIN E. (1993). *Learning sequences in music*. Chicago: GIA Publications, Inc. (Chapter 13, Measurement and Evaluation in Music).

GRONLUND, NORMAN E., and ROBERT LINN. (1990). *Measurement and evaluation in teaching*, 6th ed. New York: Macmillan.

Appendix A: Songs Categorized By Range

RANGE OF DO-MI:

At Pierrot's Door (no B section)

Hot Cross Buns

Mary Had a Little Lamb (change *sol* to *mi*)

RANGE OF DO-SOL:

Deaf Woman's Courtship

Go Tell Aunt Rhody

Jingle Bells (chorus)

Lightly Row

O Come Little Children

Oats, Peas, Beans

Ode to Joy Theme (Beethoven's 9th Symphony)

Going Home Theme (Dvorak's "New World" Symphony)

When Day Is Done

When the Saints Go Marching In

RANGE OF LA-MI:

Hey, Ho, Nobody Home (round)

RANGE OF DO-LA:

A Tisket, A Tasket

Baa, Baa, Black Sheep

For He's a Jolly Good Fellow

Hickory, Dickory, Dock

Kum Ba Ya

London Bridge

Lovely Evening (round)

Michael, Row the Boat Ashore

Oh, Susanna

Old Time Religion

Rock-a My Soul

This Old Man

Twinkle, Twinkle Little Star

Up on the Housetop

Way Down Yonder in the Pawpaw Patch

RANGE OF SOL-MI:

Jolly Old St. Nicholas

Little Brown Church in the Valley

Old McDonald

Tom Dooley

RANGE OF SOL-FA:

Aura Lee

Bingo

RANGE OF DO-DO:

Camptown Races

Deck the Halls

Drink to Me Only

Hail, Hail, The Gang's All Here

Kookaburra (round)

Little Tom Tinker

Marines Hymn

Oh Dear, What Can the Matter Be?

On Top of Old Smoky
Over the River and Through the Woods
Ring, Ring the Banjo
Row, Row, Row Your Boat
The First Noel
Three Blind Mice

    RANGE OF SOL-SOL:
Amazing Grace
Are You Sleeping?
Clementine (chorus)
Down in the Valley
Home on the Range
Let Us Sing Together (round)
Long, Long Ago
Oh Tannenbaum
Old Hundredth (The Doxology)

    RANGE OF MI-MI:
My Bonnie
When Johnny Comes Marching Home

Appendix B: Triple Meter Songs

The following list of song titles is representative of available melodies, many from folk music, that have an underlying triple meter feeling (pat-clap-clap).

Amazing Grace

The Ash Grove

The Band Played On

Barbara Allen

Blow the Man Down

Campbells Are Comin'

Carnival of Venice

Cielito Lindo

Cockles and Mussels

Daisy, Daisy

Did You Ever See a Lassie?

Dona Nobis Pacem (round)

Drink to Me Only with Thine Eyes

Eency Weency Spider

The Farmer in the Dell

The First Noel

Flow Gently Sweet Afton

For He's a Jolly Good Fellow

Goober Peas

Goodbye, Old Paint

Greensleeves
Hey Diddle Diddle
Hickory, Dickory, Dock
Hole in the Bucket
Home on the Range
In the Good Old Summertime
Lavender's Blue
Lazy Mary
Little Jack Horner
Little Tom Tinker
Looby Loo
The Man on the Flying Trapeze
The Mulberry Bush
My Bonnie
Oats, Peas, Beans
Oh Dear, What Can the Matter Be?
Oh, How Lovely Is the Evening (round)
On Top of Old Smoky
Over the River and Through the Woods
Pop Goes the Weasel
Ring Around the Rosy
Rock-a-Bye Baby
Row, Row, Row Your Boat
Sailing, Sailing
Scarborough Fair
The Sidewalks of New York
Silent Night
So Long, It's Been Good to Know You
Streets of Laredo
Summer Is a-Comin' In (round)
Sweet and Low
Sweet Betsy from Pike

Take Me Out to the Ball Game

Three Blind Mice

Vive La Compagnie

We Gather Together

We Three Kings of Orient Are

We Wish You a Merry Christmas

When Johnny Comes Marching Home

Where, Oh Where Has My Little Dog Gone

Whoopee Ti Yi Yo

Index